España Viva

ACTIVITY BOOK

España Viva
ACTIVITY BOOK

María Assumpta Serarols

BBC Books

Published by BBC Books,
a division of BBC Enterprises Limited,
Woodlands, 80 Wood Lane, London W12 0TT

First published 1990
This edition published 1993
© María Assumpta Serarols 1990

ISBN 0 563 36076 3

Designed by Tim Higgins
Illustrations © Kate Simunek 1990
Set in Itek Palatino by
Ace Filmsetting Ltd, Frome, Somerset
Printed and bound in Great Britain by
Ebenezer Baylis & Son Ltd, Worcester
Cover printed by Clays Ltd, St Ives plc, England

Contents

Introduction: How to use the book

This book follows the *España Viva* course book closely and its aim is to provide further practice of all the grammar points covered by the course. One of the main objectives is to encourage you to produce accurate Spanish that could be heard in real life, rather than work through artificial drills. The 15 units correspond in title and content to those in the main course book and the exercises relate to structures encountered there. The course book explains these grammar points principally in the sections *How Spanish Works*, although a few exercises are based on points touched on in *Spanish Live*. At the end of this book you will find a list of the grammar points covered, along with references to the exercises which practise each point. The points are arranged in logical order, beginning with the basic rules of the language.

A few of the exercises provide an opportunity to use idioms or vocabulary rather than practise a specific grammar point and are included when a particular area of vocabulary is central to the unit in the course book. Some exercises relate to very general aspects of grammar such as word order. Others will help you to make the right connections between chunks of language and will improve your grasp of meaning. Unit 15, the longest in the book, is devoted to revision tasks. Exercises dealing with a specific grammar point begin with a brief summary and most have a page reference to the course book explanation. An example of what you are expected to do in each exercise is provided if the aim of the task is not immediately clear.

The words used are mostly to be found in the *España Viva* course book: those which are not are listed under *New Words* at the beginning of each unit and included in the Glossary at the end of the workbook. If you come across an unfamiliar word you will find it in the Vocabulary or Word Groups at the end of the course book. The word may have appeared in one of the dialogues in the unit, so it is worthwhile reading through them carefully before you start the exercise.

At the end of this workbook there is a key to the exercises: where a single word or letter is sufficient to make the answer clear, lengthier forms are not given. There is also a short multiple-choice test on what you have learned: the scoring system and comments should help you to assess how much progress you have made. So good luck or, better still, *¡buena suerte!*

Unit 1 *¿Cómo te llamas?*

1 There are two words for *you* in Spanish: **tú** and **usted**. The verb ending changes according to which one you use (see *España Viva* course book p 18).

The following questions are unfinished. Choose a word or words from the box below to complete them:

a ¿De dónde _eres_ tú?

b ¿ _tú_ eres de Zaragoza?

c ¿Cómo _se llama_ usted, por favor?

d Y tú, ¿cómo _te llamas_?

e Y usted, ¿de _dónde es_?

f ¿Por favor, _es_ usted de Gerona?

g ¿Se llama _usted_ Pedro Zapater?

se llama
te llamas
eres
es
tú
usted
dónde es

2 To say where you come from you use **soy/eres/es** followed by **de** or an adjective of nationality (see *España Viva* course book p 18).

Select an answer to each question from the right hand column:

EXAMPLE **¿De dónde eres?**   **Yo soy de Londres**

a ¿De dónde eres?
b ¿De dónde es usted?
c ¿Eres española?
d ¿Es usted inglés?
e Yo soy argentina, ¿y usted?
f ¿Eres de aquí?
g ¿Eres extranjera?

1 Sí, soy de Toledo.
2 No, no soy de aquí. Soy andaluz.
3 Yo también soy latinoamericana, pero soy del Perú.
4 Yo soy de Londres.
5 No, soy de Dublín, soy irlandés.
6 No, soy española.

3 Rearrange the following sentences putting the words in the correct order:

EXAMPLE **¿catalana usted es?** -----> **¿Es usted catalana?**

a ¿llamas te cómo?   ¿ _Cómo te llamas_ ?

b ¿aquí de eres?   ¿ _Eres de aquí_ ?

c ¿usted dónde de es?   ¿ _De dónde es usted_ ?

d ¿cómo señorita llama se?   ¿ _Cómo se llama s_ ?

e no de yo Londres soy.   _Yo no soy de Londres_

f ¿usted alemana es?   ¿ _Es usted alemana_ ?

4 The form of the verb changes depending on the person to whom you are speaking.

How quickly can you spot whether these speakers are using **usted** or **tú**? Tick the form of *you* used in each question:

a ¿Eres galesa?   usted   tú
b ¿De dónde eres?   usted   tú
c ¿Es escocés?   usted   tú
d ¿Cómo te llamas?   usted   tú
e ¿Eres de Valencia?   usted   tú

5 Look at the following verbs. Each one should contain a complete verb. Decide whether you need to add **-s**, **-es**, or nothing (ø):

a ¿Cómo te llama_s_ ?
b ¿De dónde es____ ?
c ¿De dónde er_es_ tú?
d Tú te llama_s_ Gómez, ¿no?
e Usted, ¿de dónde_es_ ?
f ¿Usted se llama____ Enrique?

6 The endings of words for nationalities vary according to gender (see *España Viva* course book p 18).

All the people on the map opposite and in the list that follows are on holiday at a Spanish resort. They introduce themselves, giving their names and saying where they are from. Finally they state their nationality.

EXAMPLE   **David: Hola. Me llamo David. Soy de Londres. Soy inglés.**

a Anne b Margaret c Penny d Roger e Paul f Marta g Frank h Mary i Ernesto

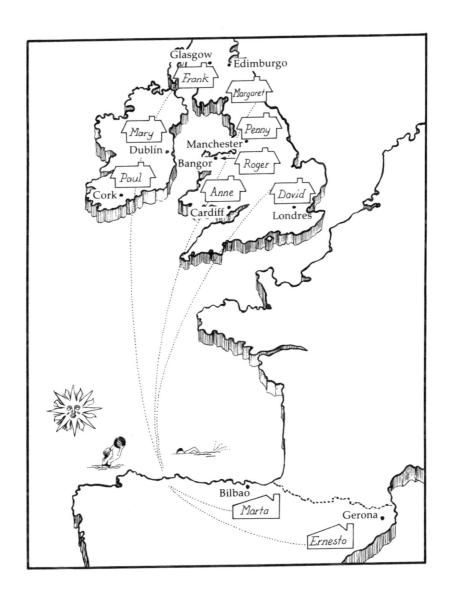

Unit 2   *¡Mucho gusto!*

---

1 All Spanish words are divided into two groups or genders, masculine and feminine. The word for *a* depends on the gender of the word that follows (see *España Viva* course book p 29).

Divide the following drinks into two lists, one masculine and one feminine, writing **un** or **una** before each one:

tónica   café   agua mineral   té   cerveza   vino   gaseosa   jerez

coca-cola   coñac   cava   gin tonic   zumo de naranja   cortado   zumo de tomate

---

2 The word for *the* also changes according to the gender of the following word.

Here is an incomplete conversation overheard in a bar where a number of people are ordering meals. Fill in the gaps with **el/la** or **un/una** as appropriate:

Camarero: Buenos días. ¿Qué van a tomar?

María: Para mí, __una__ cerveza, por favor.

Luis: Para mí, __un__ vino tinto.

Juan: __un__ vino, ¿es español?

Camarero: ¡Claro!

Juan: Para mí, __un__ vino blanco, entonces.

Camarero: ¿Y usted?

Esteban: Yo quiero __un__ té.

Camarero: Entonces, __una__ cerveza, __un__ vino tinto, __un__ vino blanco y __un__ té. ¿Quiere __un__ té con leche?

Esteban: No, con limón.

Camarero: Ahora mismo.

---

3 At another table, the waiter can't remember who ordered what:

Camarero: ¿ __una__ tónica?

Señora: Para mí, por favor.

Camarero: ¿Y __un__ zumo de tomate?

Señorita: Para mí.

Camarero: ¿Y __un__ café con leche?

Señor: Para mí.

4 Remember that words referring to people also have a masculine and feminine form.

Here are some people being introduced to each other. Rewrite what is said, changing the gender of the words in bold:

Introduction:	*Response:*
a Te presento a Juan.	**Encantado.** *Encantada*
b **Éste** es mi **amigo**. *ésta amiga*	Hola, ¿qué tal?
c **Ésta** es **la hermana** de mi **vecino**. *el hermano vecina*	Mucho gusto.
d Te presento a mi **novio**. *novia*	**Encantada.** *Encantado*
e Mi **cuñada** es **inglesa** de Coventry. *cuñado inglés*	Hola ¿cómo está?
f **Ésta** es **la tía** de Fernando. *tío*	Mucho gusto.
g **Ésta** es mi **mujer**. *marido*	¿Qué tal, cómo estás?
h Te presento a mi **madre**. *padre*	Mucho gusto.

5 Question words (¿**qué**? ¿**cómo**?) usually come at the beginning of a sentence and are a clue to what the question is about (see *España Viva* course book p 185).

Here is a series of short exchanges. The replies to the questions and introductions are listed in random order in the right hand column. Choose a suitable reply to each remark. Remember that some of them can be used twice.

a ¿Qué quieres, té o café? ___2___   1 Mucho gusto.

b ¿Cómo estás? ___3___   2 Para mí, té.

c Te presento a mi familia ___1___   3 Muy bien, gracias.

d ¿Qué tal? ___3___   4 Muchas gracias.

e Ésta es mi novia ___1___

f ¿Qué tomas? ___2___

6 There are two words for *this*, depending on the gender of the person whom you are introducing (see *España Viva* course book p 29).

Here is José introducing his family. Fill in the gaps with **éste** or **ésta** as appropriate:

Te presento a mi familia. ___ésta___ es mi madre, Teresa, y ___éste___ es mi padre, Ernesto. Y ___éste___ es mi hermano, Luis y su mujer, Mercedes. Y ___ésta___ es mi hermana, Lola y su hijo Francisco, con un amigo, Tomás. Y ___ésta___ es la novia de Francisco, se llama Inés.

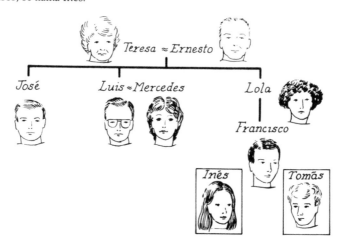

Unit 3   *De compras*

1 The plural of words is formed by adding **-s** or **-es** to the ending (see *España Viva* course book p 40).

Rewrite the following words in the plural. They are all types of food.

a queso _____ *queso*

b pan _____ *panes*

c jamón _____ *jamones*

d lechuga _____ *lechugas*

e patata _____ *patatas*

f aceituna _____ *Aceitunas*

g huevo _____ *huevos*

h plátano _____ *plátanos*

i melón _____ *Melónas*

j tomate _____ *tomates*

2 **El/la** change to **los/las** in the plural (see *España Viva* course book p 40).

The following phrases refer to different relationships between people. Rewrite each phrase in the plural:

a El hijo de Mercedes _____ *los hijos*

b El amigo de Ana _____ *los amigos*

c La hermana de Pablo _____ *las hermanas*

d La amiga de Paco _____ *las amigas*

e El primo de Juana _____ *los primos*

f La sobrina de Luisa _____ *las sobrinas*

3 Verb endings change according to the person to whom they refer (see *España Viva* course book p 40).

Look at the list of relationships in the previous exercise. Answer the following questions about the people concerned:

EXAMPLE   **¿Quién tiene un hijo?** - - - - -> *Mercedes **tiene** un hijo.*

a ¿Quién tiene un primo? _____ *Juana tiene un primo*

b ¿Y una hermana? _____ *Pablo tiene una hermana*

c ¿Y una sobrina? _____ *Luisa tiene -*

d ¿Y un hijo? _____ *Mercedes tiene*

e ¿Y una amiga? _____ *Paco tiene -*

f ¿Y un amigo? _____ *Ana ''*

4   In exercise 2 you were given a list of six relationships. However, the people referred to were not named. Use the additional information given below to identify the names of the six people referred to:

EXAMPLE

> ¡Hola! Me llamo Marta.
> Tengo un hermano.
> Se llama Pablo.

- - - - ->   **La hermana de Pablo** *se llama Marta.*

> ¡Hola! Me llamo Isabel.
> Tengo una tía.
> Se llama Luisa.

> ¡Hola! Me llamo Jorge.
> Tengo una amiga.
> Se llama Ana.

> ¡Hola! Me llamo Marisa.
> Tengo un amigo.
> Se llama Paco.

> ¡Hola! Me llamo Javier.
> Tengo una prima.
> Se llama Juana.

> ¡Hola! Me llamo Roberto.
> Mi madre se llama
> Mercedes.

a El hijo de Mercedes ___se llama Roberto___

b El amigo de Ana ___Se llama Jorge___

c La hermana de Pablo ___Se llama___

d La amiga de Paco _____

e El primo de Juana _____

f La sobrina de Luisa _____

5 Normally you don't need a word for *some* or *any* in Spanish (see *España Viva* course book p 40).

Look at the following statements and questions which you might hear in a Spanish market. Some of the Spanish sentences are incomplete. Add any words that you think are necessary in order to make the Spanish match the English sentences in brackets:

a ¿Tienen tomates maduros? *les*   (*Do you have any ripe tomatoes?*)
     un medio kilo de

b Póngame patatas, por favor   (*Half a kilo of potatoes please*)
     Algo de

c Quiero queso manchego   (*I'd like some La Mancha cheese*)
     una

d También quiero lechuga   (*I'd also like a lettuce*)

e ¿Tiene pan?   (*Do you have any bread?*)
     dos

f Póngame jamón de York y botellas de agua   (*¼ kilo of ham and 2 bottles of water*)

— *un quarto kilo de*

6 Describing words (adjectives) usually come after the word they describe (see *España Viva* course book p 40).

Add the following adjectives to appropriate items in the shopping list below:

> serrano pequeña fritas manchego
> frescas maduros grandes desnatado

(pequeñas)

a una botella de leche ___ desnatado

b ½ kilo de queso ___ Manchego

c 1 kilo de plátanos ___ Maduros

d dos latas de sardinas ___ frescas

e una bolsa de patatas ___ fritas

Grandes

f 2 tónicas ___ Grandes

g 100 gramos de jamón ___ serrano

h un yogur ___ desnatado

7 In Spanish the idea of age is expressed using the verb **tener** (*to have*). The verb ending changes according to the subject.

Here are some questions and answers about people's ages. Fill in the gaps with the appropriate form of the verb **tener**:

a ¿Cuántos años _tiene_ tu padre?

b ¿Cuántos años _tienes_ tú, María?

c Yo _tengo_ veinticinco años.

d Mis hijos _tienen_ doce y catorce años.

e ¿Solamente _tienes_ diez años? ¡Eres muy alto!

f Señorita, ¿_tiene_ usted más de 18 años?

8 Look at the list of numbers on page 205 of the *España Viva* course book.

You are helping a Spanish friend with the preparations for a party. Write in words the numbers that appear in the list of items below:

a 20 platos ___ veinte

b 5 barras de pan ___ cinco

c 2 latas de aceitunas ___ dos

d 100 servilletas de papel ___ cien

e 250 gramos de queso ___ dos cientos cincuenta

f 1 paquete de café ___ un

g 400 gramos de jamón ___ cuatro cientos

h 10 cuchillos ___ Diez

i 12 botellas de vino ___ doce

j 1.800 pesetas para un regalo ___ mille ocho cientas

Unit 4 ¿Dónde?

NEW WORDS
lo siento *I'm sorry*

---

1 **Está/están** mean *is* and *are*. They are used when saying where people and things are (see *España Viva* course book p 50).

Write the appropriate questions for the answers that follow. All the questions might be asked by someone who is seeking directions:

EXAMPLE   **¿La plaza de Tetuán? Es la primera a la izquierda.**
----->   **¿Dónde está la plaza de Tetuán, por favor?**

a ¿El Hotel Calatrava? Todo recto y la primera a la derecha. _Donde esta_

b ¿La plaza mayor? Al final de esta calle. _____

c Enfrente del supermercado está la farmacia. _____

d Coja la segunda calle a la izquierda y siga hasta la plaza. Allí está la oficina de turismo. _____

e ¿Los servicios? Lo siento, no hay. _Donde están_

f ¿Los jardines públicos? Siga todo recto. Están en las afueras, muy lejos de aquí.
Donde están

---

2 Prepositions are words which relate one noun to another. Some are used to indicate position (see *España Viva* course book p 187).

Here is a map of a street in the centre of a Spanish town which a friend has given you. She has also written some instructions to help you find your way to the park, with the help of a number of landmarks. Work out your route on the map and then fill in the prepositions which have been left out in the instructions:

1 Oficina municipal de turismo
2 Garaje 'El Tango'
3 Piso de Lourdes
4 Hotel Nuria
5 Plaza de Monserrat
6 Jardines del Mirlo

Siga _por_ la calle Calabria y ___a___ la derecha está la oficina municipal _de_ turismo. Enfrente _de_ la oficina hay un garaje. _En_ la segunda calle ___a___ la izquierda está el piso _de_ mi amiga. Enfrente _de_ su piso está el hotel y todo recto, llega usted ___a___ la plaza. _A_ diez minutos andando está el parque, ___a___ un kilómetro, más o menos.

3 **De** can mean both *of* and *from* in English (see *España Viva* course book p 50).

How would say the following in Spanish?

Ask for:

a a bottle *of* milk _una botella de leche_

b half a kilo *of* apples _un medio kilo de manzanas_

Say that:

c it's at the end *of* the street _Esta al final de la calle_

d Alejandro is *from* Peru _A es del Perú_

e Toledo is 70 kilometres *from* Madrid _T. está a de Madrid setenta k's_

4 There are two words for *is*: **es** and **está** (see *España Viva* course book p 50).

Fill in the gaps in the following conversation with either **está** or **es**:

a Perdone, ¿dónde _está_ el museo de la ciudad, por favor?

b Y usted. ¿de dónde _es_ ?

Soy de Manchester.

c El parque, ¿ _está_ lejos?

No, _está_ a unos cinco minutos en coche.

d ¿Y el centro de la ciudad?

Está muy cerca, todo recto. ¿ _Es_ usted de aquí?

No, soy extranjero.

e ¿Cómo _está_ tu amigo inglés?

Muy bien, gracias.

5 As we have seen, verb endings change according to the subject. However some endings can refer to a number of different subjects (see *España Viva* course book p 50).

Read the following sentences and identify who is the subject. (In some cases more than one subject is possible.)

EXAMPLE   **¿Dónde vives?**   yo (**tú**) él ella usted

a ¿Tu hermano vive aquí?   yo tú (él) ella usted

b ¿Vive en un piso?   yo tú él ella (usted)

c ¿Tienes amigos en España?   yo (tú) él ella usted

d ¿Cómo se llama tu novia?   yo tú (él ella) usted

e ¿Cuántos años tiene?   yo tú (él) ella (usted)

f Vivo en una casa vieja. ¿Y tú?   (yo) tú él ella usted

g ¿En qué barrio vive, señor?   yo tú él ella (usted)

6   Arrange the following groups of words so that they form a sentence. If you succeed, you will have managed to give a series of directions. To help you, the beginning and end of some of the directions have been provided.

a   primera hotel el derecha la a final a la coja está la calle izquierda y al

Coja la primera _Calle a la_ _____ el hotel.

b   oficina la la la cien catedral está turismo de de a en metros plaza enfrente

La catedral _____ de turismo.

c   izquierda coja está calle todo el la recto la derecha segunda a a bar la y

Coja la _____ izquierda.

d   aquí no lo siento de soy

Lo siento, no soy de aquí

e   veinte andando a el museo está minutos

el museo esta a veinte minutos andando

f   cerca centro la estación turismo está en la el de oficina de

la oficina de turismo esta en el centro cerca de la estacion

Unit 5   *De vacaciones*

NEW WORDS
pintoresco/a   *picturesque*   **el «rock»**   *Rock 'n Roll*

---

1   **Estar** is used to say what someone *is doing* at a particular time (see *España Viva* course book p 60).

Answer the question **¿Estás de vacaciones?** on the basis of the information given about yourself in brackets:

a _____   (*yes, you are*)

b _____   (*no, you are studying*)

c _____   (*yes, you're going for a walk*)

d _____   (*no, you're working*)

e _____   (*yes, you're sunbathing*)

f _____   (*yes, but you're learning Spanish*)

---

2   Now use the same pattern, but this time answer the questions about what *other people* are doing. The activities are the same as those given in brackets in the previous exercise.

EXAMPLE   *a* **¿Qué hace tu amigo?** - - - - -> *Está de vacaciones.*

b ¿Qué hace José?   _____

c ¿Qué hace tu amigo?   _____

d ¿Qué hace María?   _____

e ¿Qué hace su hermana?   _____

f ¿Qué hace mi madre?   _____

---

3   To say how well someone does something adverbs such as **bastante bien/un poco/muy mal** are used (see *España Viva* course book p 187).

Below is a checklist of a number of activities along with the degree of skill with which they are performed by particular individuals, as indicated by ticks and crosses in brackets:

(√√√√)   muy bien   (✕✕✕)   muy mal
(√√√)   bien   (✕✕)   mal
(√√)   bastante bien   (✕)   bastante mal
(√)   regular

Use these adverbs to say how well (or badly!) the following skills are performed:

a Hablo italiano   (√√) _____

b Bailo el «rock»   (✕✕✕) _____

c Marta toca el piano (√√√√) _____

d Hablo inglés   (✕) _____

e Mi hermano nada   (√) _____

f Mi amiga canta   (✕✕) _____

4 Now tell the truth! Say how well *you* really do these activities:

   a ¿Qué tal hablas italiano?   Hablo italiano _____

   b ¿Qué tal bailas el «rock»?   _____

   c ¿Qué tal tocas el piano?   _____

   d ¿Qué tal hablas inglés?   _____

   e ¿Qué tal nadas?   _____

   f ¿Qué tal cantas?   _____

5 **No** has two meanings: *no* and *not* (see *España Viva* course book p 60).

   Change the answers to the following questions by making them negative:

   EXAMPLE **¿Vives aquí?**
            Sí, vivo aquí. -----> **No, no vivo aquí.**

   a ¿Estás trabajando en esta oficina?
        Sí, estoy trabajando aquí.   -----> _____

   b ¿Hablas bien el francés?
        Sí, hablo francés bien.   -----> _____

   c ¿Tienes hijos?
        Sí, tengo hijos.   -----> _____

   d ¿Vives en un piso?
        Sí, vivo en un piso.   -----> _____

   e ¿Estás de vacaciones?
        Sí, estoy de vacaciones este mes. -----> _____

   f ¿Eres español?
        Sí, soy español.   -----> _____

6 The Spanish verb *to like* is **gustar** and it is used with pronouns such as **me/te/le** (see *España Viva* course book pp 60, 185).

   Fill in the gaps in the following sentences with **me/te/le** as appropriate. The person is indicated in brackets.

   EXAMPLE   ____ **gusta mucho la playa** (*I*) -----> *me* **gusta mucho la playa**

   a ¿ ____ gusta esta ciudad? (*you, formal*)

   b Sí, ____ gusta muchísimo. (*I*)

   c ¿ ____ gustan los vinos españoles? (*you, less formal*)

   d ¿ ____ gusta el paisaje de esta región? (*you, less formal*)

   e ____ gustan las vacaciones en el campo (*I*)

   f ¿ ____ gusta la comida catalana? (*you, formal*)

7 The endings of **gusta/gustan** depend on the number of things referred to (see *España Viva* course book pp 60, 185).

   Fill in the gaps in the following sentences with the correct form of **gustar**:

   a Me _____ bastante las playas mediterráneas.

   b Me _____ mucho las vacaciones junto al mar.

   c Me _____ el aire libre.

   d Me _____ un poco la montaña.

   e Me _____ los idiomas.

   f Me _____ las excursiones al campo.

   g Me _____ España.

8 The endings of adjectives must agree with the nouns they describe (see *España Viva* course book p 60).

Complete the sentences on the left with the words taken from the box, changing the endings of the adjectives as appropriate:

EXAMPLE **Me gusta esta región** - - - - -> **porque es muy bonit*a*.**

a   Vivo en un piso _____ .

b   ¿Dónde están esos pueblos _____ ?

c   ¿Tienen vino _____ ?

d   Santander es una ciudad _____ .

e   Me gusta el mar _____ .

f   Me gustan las vacaciones _____ .

g   ¿Habla idiomas _____ ?

extranjer__
modern__
tranquil__
muy limpi__
porque son divertid__
pintoresc__
tint__ barat__

Unit 6 *En coche*

NEW WORDS
el fuego *light*   **la taza** *cup*
el pastel *cake*   **útil** *useful*
la plaza mayor *main square*

---

1 **Hay** means both *there is* and *there are* and can be used both in questions and statements (see *España Viva* course book p 66).

Fill in the gaps in the following sentences with **hay/está/están**:

EXAMPLE   **¿*Hay* una gasolinera por aquí?**
-----> **¿Dónde *está* la gasolinera?**

a ¿ _____ lejos la playa?

b ¿Dónde _____ los servicios, por favor?

c ¿ _____ un aparcamiento cerca?

d Aquí _____ muchas playas limpias.

e Aquí _____ la plaza mayor.

f El museo _____ al lado del parque.

---

2 The preposition **de** is used to say what something is made of or what it contains (see *España Viva* course book p 69).

Using **de**, link each word on the left hand side with one in the box to make up something that you can eat or drink:

a un bocadillo _____

b un vaso _____

c un helado _____

d una taza _____

e una botella _____

f una ración _____

g un pastel _____

| tuti fruti |
| chocolate |
| té |
| jamón |
| patatas fritas |
| vino tinto |
| leche |

---

3 Fill in the gaps in the following dialogues:

En la calle

A: Perdone, ¿ _____ una gasolinera _____ aquí?

B: No lo sé, lo siento, no soy _____ aquí.

A: Perdone, ¿hay _____ gasolinera cerca?

C: Sí, _____ doscientos metros.

A: ¿ _____ está exactamente?

C: _____ la primera _____ a la derecha, _____ delante del banco.

En la gasolinera

A: Lleno, por favor . . . ¿ _____ planos _____ la ciudad?

D: Sí, _____ la tienda, al lado _____ los servicios.

4   When asking for things in shops, you can use **hay** instead of **tiene/tienen** (see *España Viva* course book p 69).

All the sentences that follow contain the verb **tener**, 'to have'. In some cases it can be replaced by **hay**. Make this change **where possible**:

EXAMPLE   *¿Tienen* **queso manchego?** - - - - - > **¿Hay queso manchego?**

a   ¿Cuántos hermanos **tiene** usted?   _____

b   **¿Tienen** manzanas?   _____

c   Yo **tengo** veinticinco años.   _____

d   Lo siento, no **tengo** jamón serrano.   _____

e   ¿**Tiene** fuego?   _____

f   ¿**Tiene** mapas de carreteras?   _____

5   When talking about what there is to see in a particular place you may also be able to use either **tener** or **hay**.

Make the necessary changes to the sentences that follow using an alternative to the verb given:

EXAMPLE   **En Santander** *hay* **playas muy limpias.**
        - - - - - >   **Santander** *tiene* **playas muy limpias.**

a   En España **hay** muchas catedrales famosas. _____

b   Madrid **tiene** restaurantes muy caros. _____

c   Esta discoteca **tiene** un ambiente muy divertido. _____

d   En esta carretera no **hay** gasolineras. _____

e   Las oficinas de turismo **tienen** mucha información útil. _____

f   En esta ciudad **hay** muchos parques muy bonitos. _____

6   Tick the most appropriate answer to the following questions:

1   ¿Eres de aquí?   a   Sí, a trescientos metros
                                b   Sí, soy española
                                c   Sí, hay uno aquí cerca

2   ¿Cómo está?   a   Muy bien, gracias
                                b   Está al lado de la playa
                                c   Encantado

3   ¿Cuántos hijos tienes?   a   Tengo cincuenta años
                                b   No tengo
                                c   Hay dos

4   ¿Vives en una casa moderna? a   Sí, en las afueras
                                b   Sí, hay un piso
                                c   No hay

5   ¿Hablas francés?   a   Estoy de vacaciones en Francia
                                b   No lo sé
                                c   Sí, un poco

6   ¿Te gusta la playa?   a   Sí, me gusta mucho
                                b   Sí, por aquí
                                c   Muchas gracias

Unit 7   *El tiempo es oro*

NEW WORDS
el/la escritor/a   *writer*

---

1   To say what time it is you use **es/son** (see *España Viva* course book p 79).

Look at the 8 clocks below and answer the question **¿qué hora es?**

a   01·45
b   10·30
c   12·05
d   01·00

e   01·20
f   11·15
g   07·50
h   03·45

---

2   **A** is used to say at what time things happen. **De** is required when you want to add AM or PM to a time (see *España Viva* course book p 79).

Look at the following information which tells you about the hours worked by a number of Spaniards in different occupations. Then answer the questions below:

EXAMPLE   **¿A qué hora empieza el trabajo el señor Mendoza?**
A las nueve de la mañana.

nombre y apellidos   *Juan José*
profesión   *Mendoza Palau*
electricista
horario de trabajo
mañana: de 9:00 a 13:00
tarde: de 16:30 a 20:30

a

nombre y apellidos   *Javier*
profesión   *Farrero Campmany*
arquitecto
horario de trabajo
mañana: de 9:30 a 13:30
tarde: de 16:30 a 19:30

b

nombre y apellidos   Lourdes
profesión   Miguel Lopez
secretaria
horario de trabajo

mañana: de 8:00 a 13:00

c

nombre y apellidos   Javier
profesión   Gómez Batista
controlador aereo
horario de trabajo

tarde: de 17:00 a 20:00

d

nombre y apellidos   María
profesión   Cruz Lapuente
médico
horario de trabajo

mañana: de 9:00 a 14:00
tarde: de 17:00 a 20:00

e

nombre y apellidos   Juan Pablo
profesión   Sierra Ríos
basurero
horario de trabajo

tarde: de 22:00 a 02:00

f

a ¿A qué hora termina el trabajo el señor Mendoza? _____

b ¿A qué hora empieza el trabajo Javier Farrero? _____

c ¿Y a qué hora termina? _____

d ¿A qué hora empieza Lourdes Miquel? _____

e ¿A qué hora empieza Javier Gómez? _____

f ¿Y a qué hora termina? _____

g ¿A qué hora empieza María Cruz? _____

h ¿Y a qué hora termina? _____

i ¿A qué hora empieza Juan Pablo Sierra? _____

3 You will have noticed that you say **por la mañana** and **por la tarde** when you do not specify a particular time (see *España Viva* course book p 79).

Now use the details about each person to answer the following questions:

EXAMPLE   **¿El señor Mendoza trabaja por la mañana?**
-----> **Sí, trabaja por la mañana y por la tarde.**

a ¿A qué hora empieza el señor Mendoza por la tarde? _____

b ¿Y a qué hora termina por la mañana? _____

c ¿Javier Farrero trabaja por la mañana? _____

d ¿Lourdes Miquel trabaja por la tarde? _____

e ¿Javier Gómez trabaja por la mañana? _____

f ¿A qué hora termina por la mañana María Cruz? _____

g ¿Juan Pablo Sierra trabaja por la mañana? _____

4 Remember that verb endings change depending on who is doing the action (see *España Viva* course book pp 79, 186).

Fill in the gaps in the following questions using the appropriate form of the verb in brackets:

EXAMPLE **¿En qué _____ tú?** (*trabajar*) - - - - -> **¿En qué trabaj*as*?**

a Y tú, ¿dónde _____? (**trabajar**)

b Yo no _____ en un banco. (**trabajar**)

c Yo _____ a las ocho y media. (**empezar**)

d ¿Qué horario _____ tú? (**tener**)

e Yo _____ a las tres. (**terminar**)

f Y usted, ¿dónde _____ por favor? (**vivir**)

g Yo _____ en el centro, en la Gran Vía. (**vivir**)

h ¿Tu hermano _____ idiomas extranjeros? (**hablar**)

i Sí, _____ inglés, francés y español. (**hablar**)

5 When talking about work and jobs you can use **trabajar** or **ser** (see *España Viva* course book p 76).

In the following sentences you are told where people work or what jobs they do. Using the vocabulary from *España Viva* course book pp 210–211, provide the information to complete each 'job description':

EXAMPLE **Trabajo en una tienda** - - - - -> **soy** *dependiente/a*

a Soy médico	trabajo en _____ _____
b Soy _____	trabajo en un colegio
c _____ _____	trabajo en el campo
d Soy enfermera	_____ _____ _____ _____
e Luis es director	trabaja en _____ _____
f María _____ _____	trabaja en una oficina
g Juan _____ _____	trabaja con material eléctrico
h Pedro es obrero	_____ _____ _____ _____
i _____ _____	yo doy clases de español

6 Some professions have a masculine and a feminine form, while others have only one form for both genders (see *España Viva* course book pp 76–77).

Indicate whether the following nouns refer to a woman, a man, or both:

electricista _____	contable _____
arquitecto _____	mujer de negocios _____
diseñador _____	escritora _____
ingeniera _____	dentista _____
jefe _____	profesor _____

Unit 8   *¡Que aproveche!*

NEW WORDS
el plato combinado   *mixed platter (as a set meal)*   **sabroso/a**   *tasty*
recomendar (*ie*)   *to recommend*   **salado/a**   *salty*
     el tráfico   *traffic*

---

1   Here are the answers to a number of questions you might hear in a Spanish
restaurant or café. Can you work out what the questions might have been?

a   Para mí, una ensalada variada por favor. _____

b   Un helado de chocolate. _____

c   Quiero una botella de vino tinto por favor. _____

d   ¡El lomo está riquísimo! _____

e   La tortilla a la paisana es una tortilla de verduras. _____

f   Hay platos combinados, y el menú del día. _____

g   Están al fondo, a la derecha. _____

h   Hay patatas, queso y aceitunas. _____

i   Para mí, un fino. _____

j   Con gas, por favor. _____

---

2   There is more than one way of ordering food and drink (see *España Viva* course book
p 85).

Ask for the following items, varying the way you phrase your order as much as
possible:

a   a portion of Spanish omelette _____

b   (for starters) vegetable soup _____

c   (as your main course) chicken and chips _____

d   (for your drink) a bottle of (still) mineral water and a beer _____

e   (for dessert) fruit _____

f   (as a main course) squid _____

g   (for your drink) a jug of water _____

h   (for dessert) pears in wine and ... the bill _____

---

3   There are two ways of saying *very*: you can use **muy** before the adjective or else add the
-ísimo endings to the adjective itself (see *España Viva* course book p 90).

Here is a series of comments made in the course of a meal in a Spanish restaurant.
Express agreement with what each person says, using adjectives with the ending
ísimo/ísima/ísimos/ísimas:

EXAMPLE   **La pasta está muy buena.**
----->   **¡Sí!, ¡está buen*ísima*!**

a La carne a la parrilla está muy buena. _____

b Los huevos fritos están muy sabrosos. _____

c La paella está muy rica. _____

d Este rape está muy salado. _____

e Estas costillas están muy cocidas. _____

f Las patatas están muy buenas. _____

g El menú es muy barato. _____

h El rape es demasiado caro. _____

i La lección es muy difícil. _____

4 Some verbs change not only at the end but in the middle as well. These are known as 'radical changing verbs' (see *España Viva* course book p 90).

Here are some common radical changing verbs. The way in which the middle vowel changes is indicated in brackets:

empezar (*ie*)   **querer** (*ie*)
preferir (*ie*)   **cerrar** (*ie*)
recomendar (*ie*)   **pensar** (*ie*)

Supply the verbs in the following sentences. The verbs are listed in random order below, but they are missing their middle vowels.

EXAMPLE   **¿A qué hora _____ el trabajo?**

- - - - -> **¿A qué hora empiezas el trabajo?**

a Yo _____ el trabajo a las ocho.

b Yo _____ un café con leche, por favor.

c ¿Qué tipo de helado _____ tú?

d ¿Cómo _____ usted el pollo? ¿A la parrilla?

e Yo _____ el pescado. No me gusta la carne.

f El restaurante _____ a las doce.

g ¿Qué _____ tú del restaurante? Es buenísimo, ¿no?

h ¿Qué _____ el camarero? ¿La paella?

pref___ro   pref___res   qu___ro   recom___nda

c___rra   qu___re   emp___zo   p___nsas

5 The following questions and answers also use these verbs. Fill in the gaps with the most appropriate form of the verb selected from the alternatives given:

1 ¿Qué _____ la señora, helado o fruta?   *a* prefiere
                                               b prefieres
                                               c prefiero

2 Señor, ¿qué _____ tomar?   *a* quiere
                                 b quieres
                                 c quiero

3 ¿Tú _____ a las ocho o a las nueve?   *a* empieza
                                            b empiezas
                                            c empiezo

4 ¿A qué hora _____ el café?   *a* cierra
                                   b cierras
                                   c cierro

5 ¿Tú _____ tomar cerveza también?   *a* piensa
                                          b piensas
                                          c pienso

6 ¿Qué vino nos _____ usted?   *a* recomienda
                                          b recomiendas
                                          c recomiendo

7 Juan, ¿qué vas a tomar de primero?
  _____ sopa de pescado.   *a* quiere
                                          b quieres
                                          c quiero

6   Here is a young Spanish woman, Mercedes Barra, telling us a few details about herself. Read what she has to say:

Me **llamo** Mercedes Barra. **Vivo** en Burgos, en un piso bastante pequeño en el centro. **Tengo** dos hijos: Ariana **tiene** cinco años y Óscar **tiene** siete. **Soy** profesora. **Trabajo** en un instituto. **Empiezo** a las diez y **termino** a las tres. **Me gusta** mucho Burgos, **es** una ciudad tranquila. **No me gustan** las ciudades muy grandes porque **no me gusta** el tráfico. En Burgos **hay** muchos restaurantes buenísimos: los platos de carne **me gustan** mucho. **No me gusta** mucho el pescado. En Burgos **hay** también muchos monumentos interesantes y una catedral muy bonita. La ciudad **tiene** un ambiente muy bueno.

Mercedes' cousin, Ignacio García, lives in Valencia. Write a similar paragraph about him using the information provided below. Try to include the verbs in bold type which Mercedes has used in her account but remember to change the endings to the 'he' form. Begin your account as follows:

El primo de Mercedes **se llama** Ignacio . . .

name:	Ignacio García Moreno
age:	35
children:	0
type of home:	Large house on the outskirts of Valencia. (Does not like the flats available in the city centre.)
profession:	Doctor (loves his work)
place of work:	Hospital (in Valencia)
hours of work:	14:00 to 22:00
interests:	Likes Valencia because it is big, interesting and lively. Enjoys eating out in the many restaurants in the city. Does not like meat. Loves fish dishes, especially paella. Speaks English and Italian. Does not like animals.

7 Remember that as well as saying what *you* enjoy or dislike, you can use **gusta** and **gustan** to talk about other people's tastes, to say what *he* or *she* likes and dislikes (see *España Viva* course book p 185).

Look at the list of possible likes and dislikes in the table below. Write out as many sentences as you can identifying who enjoys and dislikes what:

EXAMPLE   **Mercedes: le gusta Burgos**
              Ignacio: no le gustan los animales

Mercedes: _____

_____

_____

_____

_____

_____

_____

_____

Ignacio: _____

_____

_____

_____

_____

_____

_____

_____

Valencia
Burgos
la paella
los pisos en el centro
las ciudades grandes
la carne
el italiano
los restaurantes
los animales
el pescado
las ciudades pequeñas

Unit 9 *De tiendas*

NEW WORDS

la bufanda *(woollen) scarf* **estampado/a** *patterned*
cómodo/a *comfortable* **las gafas de sol** *sunglasses*
elegante *smart, elegant* **el pañuelo** *handkerchief, (fine) scarf*
entonces *then* **precioso/a** *very pretty*

---

1 To ask someone for an opinion, or express your own, you use **¿qué te parece?/¿qué le parece?/me parece** (see *España Viva* course book p 101).

Express your opinion using **me parece** followed by an appropriate adjective from the list below:

EXAMPLE **¿Te gusta este bolso?**
-----> **Sí, me parece** *precioso*

a ¿Te gustan estos zapatos?

Sí sí, _____

b ¿Qué le parece esta camisa?

Me gusta mucho, _____

c ¿Cuánto vale este pañuelo de seda?

Veinte mil pesetas.

¡Veinte mil pesetas! ¡ _____ !

d ¿Qué talla es esta chaqueta?

La talla 40.

¿La talla 40? _____

e ¿Le gustan estas corbatas?

Son de seda, ¿no? _____

f ¿Estos pantalones le parecen caros?

No no, _____

baratos
muy cómodos
pequeña
caro
muy elegante
muy bonitas
precioso

---

2 The choice between **¿qué te parece?** and **¿qué le parece?** depends on whether you are using **tú** or **usted** (see *España Viva* course book p 101).

Look at the sentences below and decide whether you would use **¿qué te parece?** or **¿qué le parece?** to find out what the person with you thinks. Be careful! If the thing you are referring to is a plural noun, you will have to use **parecen**.

a ¿Te gusta esta bufanda? ¿Qué _____ ?

b ¿Quiere probarse estos pantalones? ¿Qué _____ ?

c ¿Qué talla tiene, señora?

No sé, ¿qué _____ ?

d ¿Te gustan estos zapatos? ¿Qué _____ ?

e ¿En qué color le gustan más los zapatos, señor? ¿Qué _____ éstos?

3 The words for *it* are **lo** and **la**; the words for *them* are **los** and **las**. The word you choose depends on the object or objects you are referring to.

The questions and comments that follow might be heard in a Spanish department store. React to each remark by saying that you'll take the item or items referred to:

EXAMPLE   **¿Le gustan estas postales?**
- - - - ->   **Sí, me *las* llevo.**

a ¿Qué le parece esta camisa en rojo?

Me gusta, _____

b ¿Te gustan estos calcetines?

Sí, _____

c ¡Este jersey es muy bonito!

Es precioso, _____

d ¿Prefiere las medias rojas o amarillas?

Las amarillas, _____

e ¿La tiene en una talla más grande?

Sí, señor.

Entonces, _____

f ¿Qué le parece este perfume?

Es caro, pero _____

g ¡Me gusta mucho este reloj!

Es muy bonito, _____

4 The articles **el/la/los/las** can be used with adjectives when referring to objects. They are used to specify *which one* (see *España Viva* course book p 100).

Here is a list of items with details of the colours etc. available. Your preference is indicated. Identify which one or ones you want:

EXAMPLE   *zapatos*   rojos (blancos) marrones negros
- - - - ->   **quiero *los blancos***

a traje de baño   azul   negro (estampado)

b vestido   (gris) blanco   azul marino

c falda   negra (blanca) amarilla

d pantalones   (blancos) grises   rojos

e gafas de sol   negras   marrones (rojas)

f camiseta   amarilla   blanca (celeste)

g jersey   (verde) estampado   otro

5 **Éste/ésta** mean *this one* (see *España Viva* course book p 100).

Look at the items below and explain why you decided to purchase each one. The reason in each case is that you think you've got a bargain.

EXAMPLE   **¿Qué camisa te llevas?**
Me llevo *ésta* porque es baratísima.

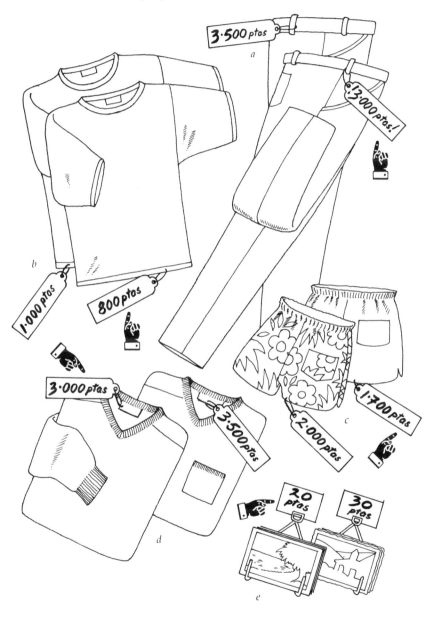

a ¿Qué pantalón te llevas? _____

b ¿Qué camiseta te llevas? _____

c ¿Qué traje de baño te llevas? _____

d ¿Qué jersey te llevas? _____

e ¿Qué postal te llevas? _____

6 To find out the times at which shops, banks etc. open and shut, use the expressions
¿a qué hora se abre? and **¿a qué hora se cierra?** (see *España Viva* course book p 99).

Look at the signs below and then study the information that follows. Work out
what questions have been asked in order to obtain the replies given:

EXAMPLE   **por la tarde no se abre**
   - - - - ->   **¿A qué hora se abre el supermercado los sábados por la tarde?**

FARMACIA	**SUPERMERCADO BONUS**	**EL DRUGSTORE**

lunes 17.00–21.00
martes–viernes
   09.00–13.30
   17.00–21.00
sábado cerrado
	lunes–viernes 08.00–13.00
	              17.30–22.30
	sábado 08.00–14.00
		sábados y domingo
		¡ABIERTO 24 HORAS!

a se cierra a las dos _____

b no se abre por la mañana _____

c se abre a las ocho _____

d no se cierra _____

e se cierra a las nueve _____

7 Look at the two columns of questions and answers below. Which answer goes
with each question?

a ¿Te parece bonito este collar?

b ¿Qué talla tiene?

c ¿Quiere probarse la chaqueta?

d ¿Tienen sellos para Inglaterra,
   por favor?

e ¿Le gusta esta falda?

f ¿Me está bien?

g ¿La tienen en otro color?

h ¿Los tienen en otra talla más grande?

1 Sí, la tengo en rojo y en blanco.

2 No, lo siento mucho.

3 Sí, me parece muy bonito.

4 La cuarenta y cuatro, por favor.

5 Sí, gracias. ¿Dónde están los
   probadores, por favor?

6 Es preciosa, me gusta mucho.

7 Un poco pequeña, ¿no te parece?

8 Sí, claro. ¿Cuántos quiere?

Unit 10   *Tiempo libre*

NEW WORDS

al día   *per day*   **enérgico/a**   *energetic*
chino/a   *Chinese*   **los juegos de mesa**   *board games*
el ejercicio   *exercise*
(many words for particular sports are the same in Spanish and English)

---

1   When talking about your hobbies you can say **soy aficionado/a**. This is followed by **a** or **al** (see *España Viva* course book p 109).

Answer the following questions about hobbies and sport as though you were the person indicated. Be careful to choose the correct ending for **aficionado**, according to the gender of the person speaking, and to use **a** or **al** as appropriate before the activity.

EXAMPLE   **¿Te gustan los deportes?**
María: Sí, soy aficionada al hockey.

1 ¿Te gustan los deportes?   *a* María: hockey _____
                                  b Esteban: golf _____
                                  c Ernesto: swimming _____

2 ¿Cuáles son tus aficiones?   *a* Teresa: reading _____
                                  b Joaquín: modern music _____
                                  c David: cooking _____

3 ¿Qué te gusta hacer en tu tiempo libre?   *a* Pepe: cinema _____
                                  b Rosa: theatre _____
                                  c Cristina: art _____

---

2   In Unit 8 you practised using **gusta** and **gustan** with different nouns in order to say what things you like and dislike (see *España Viva* course book p 185). You can also use **gusta** with a verb to talk about activities that you enjoy or dislike. The verb that follows **gusta** will always end in **-r**.

Use the table below to talk about the activities that you enjoy or dislike doing in your free time:

EXAMPLE   **no me gusta . . . jugar al tenis**

me gusta		vivir en una ciudad grande
		trabajar por la mañana
no me gusta	(mucho)	comer en restaurantes buenos
		hablar idiomas extranjeros
		jugar al tenis
		hacer este curso de español
		coleccionar sellos
		practicar deportes
		ver la televisión
		escuchar música
		nadar en el mar

3   **Prefiero** can be also used with another verb in order to express a preference (see *España Viva* course book p 109).

Look at the following pairs of activities. Each activity is given a 'star' rating to indicate how much you enjoy it. Make up statements indicating your preferences:

EXAMPLE   **jugar al golf (★★★★★)   jugar al tenis (★★★★)**
-----> *Me gusta mucho* **jugar al tenis, pero** *prefiero* **jugar al golf.**

a   comer en casa (★★★★★)   comer en un restaurante (★★★) _____

b   nadar en el mar (★★★★)   nadar en la piscina (★★★★★) _____

c   hablar italiano (★★)   hablar español (★★★) _____

d   ir al teatro (★★★)   ir al cine (★) _____

e   escuchar música (★★★★★)   bailar (★★★) _____

f   leer novelas (★★★★)   leer revistas (★★) _____

4   To say that you are *going to do* something, use **voy a** followed by the **-r** part of the verb (the infinitive).

The following sentences tell you what a number of people normally do in their spare time. Use the information provided to say what they are *going to do* at the time indicated:

EXAMPLE   **Cuando estoy libre, casi siempre escucho música clásica.**
(¿esta tarde?)
-----> **Esta tarde** *voy a escuchar* **música clásica.**

a   Cuando estoy libre, casi siempre leo novelas. (**¿esta tarde?**) _____

b   ¿Cocinas si tienes tiempo? (**¿esta noche?**) _____

c   María Cubells hace footing. (**¿hoy?**) _____

d   A veces hago atletismo. (**¿esta mañana?**) _____

e   ¿Vas a alguna exposición? (**¿esta semana?**) _____

f   Me gusta comer en este restaurante chino. (**¿hoy?**) _____

g   Soy aficionada a la natación. (**¿esta tarde?**) _____

5   In Unit 8 you met a number of verbs whose middle vowels changed (see *España Viva* course book p 109). Some verbs change their middle vowels from **o** to **ue**.

Write the appropriate form of the verbs in brackets in the person indicated:

a   _____ (**dormir, yo**) la siesta cuando _____ (**poder**).

b   ¿ _____ (**jugar, tú**) al ajedrez cada semana?

c   Y usted, ¿ _____ (**poder**) practicar muchos deportes en su tiempo libre?

d   ¿A qué hora _____ (**volver, tú**) a casa después del trabajo?

e   Yo _____ (**volver**) a las siete y media.

f   ¿Cuánto _____ (**costar**) este libro?

g   Yolanda sólo _____ (**dormir**) seis horas al día.

h   ¿Cuánto _____ (**costar**) hacer un curso de natación?

6 To say that you play a particular sport, use the verb **jugar a/al** (see *España Viva* course book p 109). Remember that **jugar** is a radical changing verb.

Read the information given below and identify what sport each person plays. The list of possible sports is given in the box:

a Marisa: es aficionada a los deportes, pero prefiere los deportes tranquilos. _____

b Juan: le gusta practicar el deporte más popular de España. _____

c Marta María: le gustan los deportes acuáticos. _____

d Jorge: prefiere un deporte enérgico. _____

e Pepa: le gusta jugar con su amiga. No le gusta jugar en un equipo. _____

f Javier: prefiere los juegos de mesa. _____

tenis   waterpolo   golf   baloncesto   ajedrez   fútbol

7 The irregular verbs tend to change in a more unpredictable way (see *España Viva* course book p 109).

Fill in the gaps in the following sentences with a verb selected from the box:

a Yo _____ una hermana en Cádiz.

b ¿Dónde _____ (**tú**) trabajando?

c No trabajo, _____ de vacaciones.

d ¿Qué _____ usted los domingos por la mañana?

e ¿De dónde _____ (**tú**)?

f ¿Tú _____ amigos en España?

g Yo _____ ejercicio en el cuarto de baño por la mañana.

h ¿ _____ usted inglesa?

hago
eres
estás
es
hace
tengo
tienes
estoy

Unit 11 *¡Buen viaje!*

NEW WORDS

a pie *on foot, walking* **largo/a** *long*
directo/a *through train* **rápido/a** *fast*

---

1 Sort out the words in each sequence to form a question connected with travel:

a ¿sale el a para hora qué tren Valencia? _____

b ¿llega plaza Gaudí se a favor cómo la por? _____

c ¿Gran Vía a este va la autobús? _____

d ¿un ida o quiere billete y de de vuelta ida? _____

e ¿de el sale dónde autobús treinta número? _____

f ¿a por hay Sevilla trenes tarde después la de seis las? _____

g ¿el verdad tren éste para Córdoba es? _____

---

2 The form of the verb for *he* and *she* is exactly the same as for **usted** (see *España Viva* course book p 120).

Fill in the gaps in the sentences below using the correct form of the verb in brackets. They all refer to **él** or **ella**:

a La hermana de Lourdes _____ **(estar)** en el sur de España trabajando.

b María José _____ **(llegar)** de Madrid esta noche.

c Enrique no _____ **(coger)** el tren: _____ **(preferir)** ir en coche.

d Conchita _____ **(salir)** con su madre los viernes.

e La vecina de Juanita _____ **(ser)** la directora de la empresa.

f Ana _____ **(tener)** sólo seis años.

g Mi amiga Merche _____ **(venir)** al trabajo a pie.

h El nieto de Montse _____ **(viajar)** mucho en avión.

---

3 The following statements are all in the first person. Rewrite them in the third person:

EXAMPLE **Tengo quince años.**   (Teresa) *tiene* **quince años también.**

a Estoy en la farmacia. José _____

b Hago mucha natación. Irene _____

c Siempre cojo el tren de las dos y cinco. María Inés _____

d Soy estudiante. mi amigo Rafa _____

e Llego a casa a las siete. Ricardo _____

f Trabajo nueve horas al día. mi profesor _____

g Vengo en tren. Fermín _____

h ¡Tengo mucho trabajo! Jorge _____

4 When using the twenty-four-hour clock simply state the hour and then the number of minutes after the hour (see *España Viva* course book p 120).

Rewrite the following times in words using the twenty-four-hour clock and then write out each time in figures:

EXAMPLE   **las dos y veinticinco de la tarde**
-----> **las catorce veinticinco (14:25)**

a las siete menos veinte de la tarde _____

b las doce y media del mediodía _____

c las seis y cinco de la mañana _____

d las ocho menos cinco de la tarde _____

e las once y cuarto de la noche _____

f las cuatro y veinticinco de la tarde _____

g las diez y dos minutos de la mañana _____

5 In the questions that follow, the first words have been removed and arranged in random order below. Select from the box an appropriate word or group of words to fill each gap and then choose a suitable answer to each question from those listed at the end:

> cómo   de dónde   a qué hora   dónde
> cuántos   cuándo   cuánto

a ¿ _____ sale el tren para Barcelona?

b ¿ _____ llega el próximo autobús?

c ¿ _____ está la parada del diecisiete, por favor?

d ¿ _____ sale el número doce?

e ¿ _____ vale un billete de ida y vuelta para Zaragoza?

f ¿ _____ billetes quiere, por favor?

g ¿ _____ se llega a la estación?

Answers

1 la primera calle a la derecha
2 aquí mismo, delante del banco
3 sale a las catorce quince
4 dos de ida y vuelta, por favor
5 llega dentro de media hora
6 1.250 pesetas
7 sale de la parada de la calle Calabria

6 Hay can be used in many contexts.

Using the information provided below, make up statements or questions using **hay**:

EXAMPLE   **tren (Madrid)** -----> **¿Hay un tren para Madrid?**

a ¿autobús (Tarragona)? _____

b ¿gasolinera (cerca)? _____

c ¿para turistas (en Ávila)? _____

d (en Tarragona) murallas antiguas? _____

e ¿farmacia (por aquí)? _____

f ¿playa limpia (en esta costa)? _____

7 The following paragraph is an account of a forthcoming trip which Ignacio García has planned. Fifteen words have been removed from the passage and placed in random order in the box below. Can you put them back where they belong?

Ignacio García (1) _____ médico y trabaja en Valencia. Le (2) _____

mucho viajar y este viernes va (3) _____ ir de viaje a Burgos

(4) _____ vive su prima Mercedes. Va a viajar en tren porque no le

(5) _____ los viajes largos (6) _____ carretera y autopista. Prefiere

(7) _____ el Talgo porque es un tren rápido (8) _____ cómodo. El

tren (9) _____ a las cinco (10) _____ la tarde y (11) _____ a

Burgos a (12) _____ once de la noche. El tren no (13) _____

directo. Ignacio (14) _____ a pasar una semana en (15) _____ de

Mercedes.

casa	coger	va	gustan	de
y	las	por	gusta	llega
donde	es	sale	a	es

Unit 12 *Cinco estrellas*

NEW WORDS

el aire puro *fresh air*
alquilar *to rent, hire*
el bolsillo *pocket*
cambiar *to change*
cerrar con llave *to lock*

el hueso *bone*
el patín *pedalo*
preparado/a *ready*
respirar *to breathe*

el ruido *noise*
servir *to serve*
(sirven *they serve)*
sin alcohol *alcohol-free or low alcohol*

---

1 The ending **-mos** tells you that the subject of the verb is *we* (see *España Viva* course book p 130).

The following sentences are in the **yo** form. Rewrite them in the **nosotros** form:

a **Tengo** el coche aquí. _____

b **Vivo** en el centro de Segovia. _____

c **Tengo** una habitación reservada. _____

d Normalmente **como** en un bar cerca del trabajo. _____

e **Soy** de Lérida pero **estoy** trabajando en Zaragoza. _____

f **Voy** a la piscina cada lunes. _____

g **Aparco** delante de casa. _____

h **Practico** el fútbol y el squash. _____

---

2 In the following questions the **ustedes** form is used (see *España Viva* course book p 130).

Answer them with the **nosotros** verb endings:

EXAMPLE　　　　　**¿Tienen piscina?**
- - - - - > 　　**Lo siento, no tenemos.**

a ¿Van a salir por la noche?

　Sí, _____

b ¿Aceptan tarjetas de crédito?

　Sí, _____

c ¿Dejan sus pasaportes por favor?

　Sí, _____

d ¿Llevan equipaje?

　No, _____

e ¿Firman, por favor?

　¿Dónde _____ ?

f ¿Son ustedes extranjeros?

　Sí, _____ irlandeses.

3   You need to find out the information indicated below. Ask the appropriate questions using the **ustedes** form:

In a restaurant

a whether they have a set menu _____

b whether they accept credit cards _____

In a hotel

c whether they have a lift _____

d whether they book coach tickets _____

On the beach

e whether they hire out pedalos _____

f where they sell drinks _____

In a bank

g whether they change foreign coins _____

h whether they open on Saturday _____

4   The following questions use a variety of *you* forms (**tú, usted, ustedes**). Read each question carefully and then tick the best answer:

EXAMPLE   **¿Tienen teléfono?**   a **Sí, tenemos dos** √
                                    b **Sí, tiene uno**
                                    c **Sí, tienes uno**

a ¿Por la noche cierran la puerta   1 No, no cierran
   principal con llave?   2 No, no cerramos
                                            3 No, no cierras

b ¿Tienen la cuenta preparada?   1 Sí, la tienes
                                            2 Aquí está
                                            3 No hay

c ¿Llevas la llave de la habitación?   1 Sí, la llevas
                                            2 Sí, la llevamos
                                            3 La llevo en el bolsillo

d ¿Quiere tomar algo?   1 Sí, quiero un zumo de tomate
                                               por favor
                                            2 Sí, queremos agua mineral sin gas
                                            3 Muy bien, gracias

e Perdone, ¿vende cerveza sin alcohol?   1 Sí, por favor
                                            2 No, lo siento
                                            3 Sí, vendes cerveza

f ¿Tiene un horario de autobuses?   1 Sí, a las seis y media
                                            2 ¿Tienen?
                                            3 Sí, ¿de qué zona?

5 **¿Se puede?** is a useful way of asking whether something is permitted or possible (see *España Viva* course book p 130).

Each of the questions that follow contains a suggestion. Change each question in order to find out whether what is suggested is possible or allowed:

EXAMPLE   **¿Fumamos?** - - - - -> **¿Se puede fumar?**

a ¿Aparcamos aquí? _____

b ¿Entramos? _____

c ¿Comemos en este parque? _____

d ¿Telefoneamos a Inglaterra desde aquí? _____

e ¿Dejamos las joyas en recepción? _____

f ¿Desayunamos en la habitación? _____

g ¿Vamos a la discoteca del hotel? _____

6 **Se** can also be used with other verbs (see *España Viva* course book p 130).

Read the following questions and statements and decide whether to add **se** to the verb or not:

EXAMPLE   **En este hotel ____ come bien.**

       ---->   **En este hotel _se_ come bien.**

a ¿ ____ tienen bocadillos?

b ¿Cómo ____ llega al metro por favor?

c Aquí ____ sirven un pescado muy bueno.

d ¿ ____ puedo hacer fotos?

e En España, ____ trabaja mucho.

f En los cines españoles no ____ fuma.

g Los supermercados ____ cierran al mediodía.

h Montse ____ cena menos en verano.

7 The two columns below list the advantages of living in the centre of towns and in the suburbs respectively. On the basis of this information, write sentences using **se** about what you can and cannot do in each area:

EXAMPLE   **En el centro de la ciudad *se puede comprar* en tiendas más baratas.**

En el centro de la ciudad

a compras en tiendas más baratas _____

b vas a muchos espectáculos _____

c trabajas cerca de casa _____

d sales de noche con frecuencia _____

e visitas monumentos y museos _____

En las afueras

f respiras aire puro _____

g juegas en calles sin tráfico _____

h descansas sin ruido _____

i sales al campo _____

j ves el paisaje _____

Unit 13 *Sol y sombra*

NEW WORDS

el atún *tuna*
el dolor de muelas *toothache*
multinacional *multinational*

el pariente *relative*
por adelantado *in advance*
el programa *programme*

---

1 To talk about the weather you often use the verb **hacer**. There are exceptions however (see *España Viva* course book p 140).

Look at the weather map of Europe below and then answer the questions that follow:

a ¿Qué tiempo hace en Madrid? _____

b ¿Hace buen tiempo en Dublín? _____

c ¿Qué tiempo hace en Londres? _____

d En Oslo, ¿hace buen tiempo? _____

e ¿Qué tiempo hace en Roma? _____

f ¿Y en Berlín? _____

2 The endings of the Spanish present tense change according to the subject (see *España Viva* course book p 140).

Fill in the gaps in the following sentences with the appropriate form of the verbs in brackets. All the verbs are regular:

a ¿A qué hora _____ (**terminar**) las clases?

b ¿Dónde _____ (**pasar**) tus vacaciones?

c ¿ _____ (**firmar**) usted por favor?

d Yo siempre _____ (**reservar**) las habitaciones por adelantado.

e Mi trabajo me _____ (**ocupar**) ocho horas al día.

f ¿Dónde _____ (**vender, ellos**) bebidas frescas?

g Yo normalmente _____ (**aparcar**) en la calle.

h ¿Cuántas horas _____ (**tomar, vosotros**) el sol?

i _____ (**visitar, nosotras**) a los parientes en España.

j ¿Ustedes _____ (**desayunar**) en casa o en un bar?

3 You have learnt how to use **estoy** to say what you *are doing*. You can also use the simple present tense to convey a very similar meaning (see *España Viva* course book p 140).

Rewrite the sentences below in the simple present tense:

EXAMPLE   **Estoy viviendo en el piso de mi madre.**
    - - - - -> *Vivo en el piso de mi madre.*

a Estamos comiendo muy bien en este restaurante. _____

b Estoy trabajando en una empresa multinacional. _____

c ¿Qué están comprando Montse y su amiga Prisca? _____

d El tren de Jerez está llegando en este momento. _____

e ¿Estáis estudiando italiano? _____

f ¿Qué programa estás mirando? _____

4 There are a number of very common verbs which are irregular in the present tense (see *España Viva* course book p 186).

The table below contains a number of mixed up sentences which use these irregular verbs. Join up as many sentences as you can by taking something from each column:

EXAMPLE   **yo**   **hago**   **muchas fotos**

yo	vamos	a las cuatro
mi marido y yo	hacen	cada día
los amigos de Juan	hago	al cine
la hermana de Javi	tenéis	excursiones a pie
tú	das	de Valencia
ustedes	estáis	el pasaporte a la policía
vosotros	son	muy simpáticos
	venimos	muchas fotos
	viene	aquí con frequencia

5   When you are feeling unwell, there are two ways of explaining what is hurting you:
me duele and **tengo dolor de** (see *España Viva* course book p 140). Note that **me duele**
becomes **me duelen** when followed by a plural.

Look at the drawing below and say what is hurting you by answering the question
¿qué te duele?

EXAMPLE   **¡me duelen todos los huesos!**

a

b

c

d

e

f

a _____

b _____

c _____

d _____

e _____

f _____

6   Using the same drawings identify each part of the body that hurts with the
expression **tengo dolor de . . .**

EXAMPLE   **tengo dolor de oídos**

a _____

b _____

c _____

d _____

e _____

7   Study the information below about the weather at different Spanish locations and, using the words **más** or **menos**, write a statement about each place:

EXAMPLE   **Madrid 29°**   **Sevilla 31°**
En Madrid hace menos calor   or   **En Sevilla hace más calor**

a La Coruña _____

   Toledo _____

b Los Pirineos _____

   Valencia _____

c Oviedo _____

   Córdoba _____

d Madrid   agosto   32° _____

           octubre   25° _____

e Londres   invierno 5° _____

   Barcelona invierno 12° _____

f Menorca _____

   Segovia _____

a La Coruña   Toledo

b Los Pirineos   Valencia

c Oviedo   Córdoba

d Madrid   Madrid
   agosto 32°   octubre 25°

e Londres   Barcelona
   invierno 5°   invierno 12°

f Menorca   Segovia

8 **Más** can also be used with an adjective to mean *more . . .* or *. . . er* (see *España Viva* course book p 140). You can compare one thing with another by adding the word **que** (e.g. **Madrid es** *más grande que* **Valencia**). **Mejor que** means *better than*.

Look at the following pairs and make comparisons using **más** _____ **que** or **mejor que**.

EXAMPLE **vestido verde 3.500ptas**
vestido rojo 5.700ptas
- - - - -> **El vestido rojo es** *más caro que* **el verde.**

a bocadillo de queso (★) _____

bocadillo de atún (★★★★★) _____

b camisa azul talla 40 _____

camisa amarilla talla 46 _____

c 100g jamón de York 180ptas _____

100g jamón serrano 400ptas _____

d restaurante 'La Concha' (★★★★) _____

restaurante 'El Toro Bravo' (★) _____

e farmacia a 200m _____

Correos a 500m _____

f Hotel Nuria (★★★★★) _____

Hotel 'El Faro' (★★) _____

g Tomás 1,80m _____

Felipe 1,75m _____

Unit 14   *Viajes y vacaciones*

NEW WORDS

el alpinismo *rock climbing*
excelente *excellent*
histórico/a *historic*
ir de camping *to go camping*
ir de excursión *to go on an outing*
ir de vacaciones *to go on holiday*

ir de viaje *to go on a trip*
la pesca *fishing*
las ruinas romanas *Roman remains*
ruso/a *Russian*
seco/a *dry*
una tormenta *storm*

1 When talking about things in the past you use a different form of the verb (see *España Viva* course book p 149).

Put all the sentences below into past time by using **el año pasado**:

EXAMPLE **Este año voy a Italia.**
- - - - - > **El año pasado *fui* a Italia.**

a Este año **estoy** de vacaciones en México. _____

b ¿Adónde **vas** este verano? _____

c **Voy** a Torremolinos. _____

d Y ¿adónde **va** Joaquín? _____

e Luisa **está** en Manresa una semana. _____

f ¿**Estás** trabajando en verano? _____

g María **va** de vacaciones en tren. _____

h ¿Cuánto tiempo **estás** en la montaña? _____

2 To be precise about when things happened in the past you need to use words like *last year* and *last month* (see *España Viva* course book p 149).

Each of the following pairs of sentences contains one statement in the present and one in the past. Complete the sentence in the past by stating *when* the event happened. The first sentence will give you the key words:

EXAMPLE **Este verano voy de viaje a Inglaterra.**
- - - - - > *El verano pasado* fui de viaje a Inglaterra.

a Este fin de semana estoy en casa estudiando.

_____ estuve en casa descansando.

b Hoy Carmen va a comprar ropa.

_____ fue a comprar comida.

c Esta semana voy al teatro con mi novia.

_____ fui al cine con mi hermana.

d ¿Este año estás en la Costa Brava con tu familia?

¿ _____ estuviste en la Costa Dorada con tus amigos?

e Este mes Lola va de excursión al campo.

_____ Lola fue de excursión a la playa.

f ¿Este verano vas de camping?

¿ _____ fuiste a un hotel?

3 In Unit 10 you learnt how to use **voy a** with the infinitive to talk about what you are planning to do in the future (see *España Viva* course book p 149).

Rewrite the sentences below using **pensar** or **querer** followed by the infinitive:

a ¿Adónde vas a ir el año que viene? _____

b Voy a ir al Perú. _____

c ¿Qué país va usted a visitar en este viaje? _____

d Voy a pasar una semana en la playa. _____

e ¿Y qué vais a hacer? _____

f Vamos a tomar el sol. _____

g ¿Vas al cine? ¿Qué vas a ver? _____

h ¿Van a viajar el próximo verano? _____

4 Group the sentences that follow according to the tense:

group 1: Present
group 2: Past
group 3: Future (plans)

a Visito muchos países de Europa como turista.
b Fui de viaje a Francia: me gustó mucho.
c Estuve quince días en Marbella.
d Pienso coger el tren.
e Vamos a pagar a la recepción.
f Tenemos dos hijos y una hija.
g ¿Hablas ruso?
h ¿Quiere venir al cine?
i ¿Cuántos días estuviste en Marruecos?
j Asunción no quiere ir a la fiesta.

5 In the following pairs of sentences two people are talking. The second speaker reacts to what has just been said by using **gustar** in the present or the past. Fill in the gaps with an appropriate form of **gustar**. The number of gaps indicates the number of missing words.

EXAMPLE   **Fui a Barcelona el año pasado.**
- - - - - >   **¿Fuiste a Barcelona?** *¿Te gustó?*

a ¿Fuiste a ver la nueva película de Saura?

Sí, pero _____ _____ _____ mucho.

b Este verano voy a Roma.

¿Vas a Roma? ¿ _____ _____ Italia?

c Mi hermano va a pasar quince días en Galicia.

¿Por qué?

Porque _____ _____ muchísimo.

  d ¿Te gustó el viaje a Salamanca?

  Sí, pero _____ _____ más Segovia.

  e Estuve sólo un día en Huelva.

  ¡Sólo un día! ¿Por qué?

  Porque _____ _____ _____ .

  f ¿Fuiste al museo del Prado ayer?

  Sí.

  ¿ _____ _____ ?

  g ¿Estuvo usted aquí en Canarias el invierno pasado?

  Sí, y _____ _____ mucho.

6 The following table lists different aspects of three regions of Spain: the North, the Pyrenees and Extremadura in the west of the country. Imagine that you have just returned from a tour of Spain and, using the information provided, say what you liked and disliked about each region:

  EXAMPLE   **Me gustó el Norte de España porque hay buenas playas.**

El Norte de España	El Pirineo	Extremadura
verde, limpio	paisaje bonito	ciudades históricas
tranquilo	buena comida	ruinas romanas
buenas playas	pesca	mucho calor
pescado excelente	alpinismo	paisaje muy seco
llueve bastante	sin ambiente por la noche	mucha miseria
tormentas	malas comunicaciones	

Unit 15 *Haciendo turismo*

NEW WORDS

la cocina vegetariana	*vegetarian food*	**poner**	*to put*
demasiados/as	*too many*	**el/la psicólogo/a**	*psychologist*
el disco	*record*	**tocar la guitarra**	*to play the guitar*
hacer la siesta	*to have a nap*		

There is no new grammar in this unit. It aims to provide further practice of the grammar points covered in units 1–14.

---

1   Fill in each gap in the dialogues below with one of the following verbs:

tiene   tienen   hay   está   están   se puede   quiere

a   ¿Para ir a la catedral por favor?

¡(1) _____ lejos de aquí! ¿(2) _____ coche?

No, no tengo.

Entonces, (3) _____ un autobús, el catorce que va a la catedral.

b   **At the Tourist Office**

¿(1) _____ planos de la ciudad?

Sí, ¿cuántos (2) _____ ?

Uno, por favor. (*looking at the map*) ¿Dónde (3) _____ los museos más importantes?

(*pointing at the map*) Aquí . . . y aquí. ¿(4) _____ un folleto?

Muchas gracias. ¿(5) _____ un restaurante típico cerca de aquí?

Sí, (6) _____ uno, pero no se abre a mediodía.

c   **In a restaurant**

¿(1) _____ comer ahora?

No, lo siento, no abrimos hasta las doce y media.

Entonces ¿(2) _____ reservar una mesa?

Sí, señor.

---

2   Complete the verbs in the following sentences by adding the appropriate ending. All the verbs are in the present.

a   Me gusta mucho este collar. Me lo llev____ .

b   Esta tienda no se cierr____ al mediodía.

c   Yo ten____ una casa cerca de la playa.

d   ¿Tien____ ustedes tarjeta de crédito?

   e ¿Viv____ vosotros en un piso o en una casa?

   f Este verano nosotros hac____ alpinismo en el Pirineo.

   g Lola empiez____ sus vacaciones la semana próxima.

   h ¿Dónde com____ vosotros?

   i ¿Volv____ nosotros al hotel?

---

3   Work out suitable questions or remarks to elicit the following responses:

   a Muy bien, gracias ¿y tú? _____

   b Me llamo Asunción Farrero. _____

   c Tengo dos hermanos. _____

   d Tienen catorce y veinte años. _____

   e Buenas tardes. _____

   f Mucho gusto. _____

   g Yo, un gin tonic. _____

   h No, nada más. _____

   i Yo soy de Madrid. _____

---

4   Fill in the gaps in the following conversation between a shopkeeper and a customer using the words in the box below:

   Cliente: _____ de manzanas, por favor.

   Dependiente: ¿Algo más?

   Cliente: Sí, _____ de queso manchego, _____ de sardinas, _____ de patatas fritas y _____ de vino blanco.

   Dependiente: ¿Eso es todo? Son _____ .

medio kilo	mil cuatrocientas pesetas	una lata
una bolsa	una botella	cien gramos

---

5   Match up the questions and answers in the following lists. They are all connected with finding your way around and travelling.

   a ¿Dónde está la parada?

   b ¿Hay una gasolinera por aquí?

   c ¿Está lejos el centro de la ciudad?

   d ¿Dónde están los servicios?

   e ¿De dónde sale el tren para Albacete?

   f ¿Es ésta la carretera de Almería?

   g ¿A qué hora sale el próximo autobús?

   h ¿Hay restaurante en este tren?

   i ¿Cuándo llega el avión de Londres?

1 No, todo recto hasta el cruce y la carretera de Almería está a la derecha.

2 Al fondo a la izquierda.

3 Sí, hay una al final de la calle.

4 No, lo siento, no hay.

5 Está enfrente del banco, a la derecha.

6 Sale de la estación de Chamartín.

7 No, a unos cinco minutos a pie.

8 A las dieciocho quince.

9 Sale dentro de diez minutos.

6 Using the information given below write as much as you can about Conchita Fuentes. Begin your account as follows:

Conchita Fuentes vive . . .

nombre:	Conchita
apellidos:	Fuentes Morelló
dirección:	Calle Picasso, 35, Vilasar (pueblo cerca de Barcelona)
edad:	37 años
familia:	casada, marido alemán (Wolfgang), una hija (Ingrid) 5 años
profesión:	psicóloga
horario de	(en casa) de 09:00 a 13:00 (lunes, miércoles, viernes) y
trabajo:	de 14:00 a 20:00 cada día
aficiones:	música clásica, tocar la guitarra y el piano, cocina vegetariana, hacer yoga, leer
otros datos:	vacaciones en Alemania, miembro de un grupo 'verde'

Now try to write something similar about yourself.

7   Write a complete sentence in answer to the following questions using the information in brackets:

EXAMPLE   **¿Cuál es tu comida favorita?** (*meat*)
-----> **Me gusta más la carne.**

a ¿Qué te gusta más, la carne o el pescado? (*fish*) _____

b ¿Qué vestido es más caro? (*the green one*) _____

c ¿En qué mes hace más frío? (*February*) _____

d ¿Quiere esta habitación? (*a cheaper one?*) _____

e ¿Cuál prefiere? (*prefer the big bag*) _____

f ¿Cuál es el mejor plato típico de la región? (*paella – better than vegetables as a starter*)

_____

g ¿Qué prefieres, el verano o el invierno? (*prefer spring*) _____

h ¿Cuándo se trabaja menos en España? (*in afternoon Spaniards have a siesta*)

_____

8   **Por** or **de**? Fill in the gaps in the following sentences, all of which refer to the time:

a Voy al trabajo a las ocho _____ la mañana.

b No estudio el sábado _____ la tarde.

c ¿Escuchas música _____ la noche?

d Voy a terminar a las doce _____ la noche.

e _____ la mañana no me gusta hablar.

f Mi primo va a llegar a las cuatro _____ la madrugada.

9   In the following sentences a number of people are saying what they *are doing*. Supply the part of the verb which is missing in each case, choosing from the box below:

a Estamos _____ unas vacaciones estupendas en este camping.

b Mis hijos están _____ del colegio en este momento.

c ¿Qué estás _____ ?

d El tren está _____ en la estación ahora.

e Pepita está _____ la calle sin mirar y viene un coche.

f ¿Dónde están ustedes _____ aquí en España?

g Estoy _____ ruso y español durante este mes.

h ¿Qué estás _____ ? ¿Coñac?

entrar
tomar
comer
vivir
salir
cruzar
pasar
aprender

10   Use **lo/la/los/las** in the following sentences to say you will take whatever is offered to you:

a ¿Le gusta este abrigo? _____

b ¿Le gustan estos zapatos? _____

c ¿Éste es mejor? _____

d ¿Qué tal la camiseta? _____

e ¿Quiere esas sandalias? _____

f ¿Te gusta este disco? ¡Es nuevo! _____

g ¿No le gusta el cinturón? _____

h ¿Le pongo el traje de baño? _____

11 The following statements and questions might be useful in a chemist's. Complete each question by asking whether they have anything for your particular ailment or need:

a Me duele el estómago. ¿Tiene algo para _____?

b Me duele la cabeza. ¿ _____?

c Ayer estuve en la playa demasiadas horas. ¿Tiene algo para _____?

d Me duele la garganta. ¿ _____?

e Tengo un niño de seis meses. Le gustan mucho el pescado y el arroz.

¿Tiene _____?

f Voy a la playa mañana. ¿Tiene _____?

12 Complete each statement or question with a phrase from the box:

a La semana que viene, yo _____

b ¿Cuándo piensa _____?

c ¿Qué _____?

d Ayer _____

e Hace dos meses, fui _____

f Cada semana mi marido y yo _____

g El año pasado _____

h ¿Cuánto tiempo _____?

```
1 practicamos deporte y paseamos.
2 de viaje a Roma y me gustó mucho.
3 estuvimos aquí tres meses.
4 pienso estudiar cinco horas al día.
5 usted volver a Escocia.
6 estuviste en Argentina.
7 fui a la oficina de turismo.
8 quieres hacer esta tarde.
```

Multiple-choice test

Tick the most appropriate response to each of the following questions or statements:

1 ¿Es usted de aquí?
   a Sí, es de aquí
   b Muy bien, gracias
   c Sí, soy de aquí, de Santander

2 ¿Eres inglesa?
   a No, soy español
   b No, soy española
   c Buenas noches

3 Éste es mi cuñado Luis
   a ¿Cómo se llama?
   b Mucho gusto
   c Hasta luego

4 ¿Tiene una bolsa por favor?
   a No, lo siento
   b ¿Cuánto es?
   c No, gracias

5 ¿El mercado, por favor?
   a La segunda calle y todo recto
   b Hay una a la derecha
   c Son las dos

6 ¿Qué le parece este vestido?
   a Me parecen caros
   b Te parece caro
   c Me gusta muchísimo

7 ¿Qué te gusta hacer en tu tiempo libre?
   a Estoy trabajando
   b Soy aficionada a los deportes de invierno
   c No me gusta

8 ¿A qué hora se cierra el restaurante?
   a Son las cuatro
   b Cierras los domingos
   c A las cuatro

9 ¿Habláis ruso bien?
   a Lo hablamos bastante bien
   b No, no se puede
   c Lo hablo regular

10 ¿Qué haces este verano?
   a Lo hago
   b Pienso ir a Mallorca
   c Fui a Cádiz con mi familia

11 ¿Te gustó esta película?
   a Sí, pero la otra es mejor
   b Sí, me la llevo
   c Sí, ¿cuánto cuesta?

12 ¿En qué trabajas?
   a Trabajas en un bar
   b Estoy de vacaciones
   c Estoy en paro

13 ¿A qué hora empieza tu mujer en la fábrica?
   a Son las diecisiete veinticinco
   b Empieza a las siete
   c Ella, no

14 ¿De qué quieres el bocadillo?
   a No tengo
   b Uno grande, por favor
   c De queso

15 ¿Qué me recomiendas en tu ciudad?
    a Me gusta mucho el barrio antiguo
    b No tenemos, lo siento
    c Sí, te recomiendo

16 ¿Dónde come normalmente?
    a Comes en un bar
    b Como en casa
    c Comen en un restaurante

17 ¿Qué le parecen estos zapatos?
    a ¿Dónde están los probadores?
    b ¿Cuánto cuesta?
    c Me los llevo

18 ¿Qué bebida prefieres?
    a Prefiero el azul
    b No me gusta
    c El vino de la casa es mejor y más barato

19 ¿Salen muchos autobuses de aquí?
    a Sí, salimos con frecuencia
    b Sí, cada media hora
    c Sí, salen a las dos

20 ¿Qué se puede hacer en tu barrio?
    a Ir al cine, bailar, pasear en el parque . . .
    b No lo puedo hacer
    c Sí, se puede

21 ¡Hola! ¿Cómo estás?
    a Soy de Coventry
    b Me duele el estómago
    c Estoy en España

22 ¿Qué tiempo hace aquí en verano?
    a Hace dos meses
    b Es frío
    c Hace mucho sol

23 ¿Adónde fuiste el año pasado?
    a Fue a Extremadura
    b Fui a Andalucía
    c Fuiste a Menorca

24 ¿Estuvo usted en Latinoamérica el
    invierno pasado?
    a Sí, estuve dos meses
    b No, no voy a ir
    c Fue en avión

25 ¿Qué pensáis hacer mañana?
    a Van a ir a la discoteca
    b Vamos a estar en casa
    c Pensamos en español

26 ¿Adónde vas?
    a Vamos a la piscina
    b Van al teatro
    c Voy al colegio

27 ¿Jugáis al baloncesto?
    a No, no te gustan los deportes
    b Sí, juego cada semana
    c Sí, jugamos a veces

28 ¿Hablas español?
    a No, muy bien
    b No muy bien
    c Sí, hablas

29 ¿Quieres venir a la playa?
    a Hoy no puedo
    b ¿Qué quiere?
    c Sí, queremos

30 ¿Qué haces?
    a Sí, hago
    b Estoy estudiando español
    c Soy inglesa

Key to exercises

A bar (/) in the answer indicates that an alternative form is also correct. Words given in brackets may be included or omitted without changing the meaning of the sentence. Where an exercise is designed to produce an open-ended response, no solution is given in the key.

Unit 1

1 *a* eres *b* tú *c* se llama *d* te llamas *e* dónde es *f* es *g* usted

2 *a* 4 *b* 4 *c* 1 *d* 5 *e* 3 *f* 2 *g* 6

3 *a* ¿Cómo te llamas? *b* ¿Eres de aquí? *c* ¿De dónde es usted? *d* ¿Cómo se llama, señorita? *e* Yo no soy de Londres. *f* ¿Es usted alemana?

4 *a* tú *b* tú *c* usted *d* tú *e* tú

5 *a* -s *b* ø *c* -es *d* -s *e* es *f* ø

6 *a* Hola. Me llamo Anne. Soy de Cardiff. Soy galesa. *b* Hola. Me llamo Margaret. Soy de Edimburgo. Soy escocesa. *c* Hola. Me llamo Penny. Soy de Manchester. Soy inglesa. *d* Hola. Me llamo Roger. Soy de Bangor. Soy galés. *e* Hola. Me llamo Paul. Soy de Cork. Soy irlandés. *f* Hola. Me llamo Marta. Soy de Bilbao. Soy española. *g* Hola. Me llamo Frank. Soy de Glasgow. Soy escocés. *h* Hola. Me llamo Mary. Soy de Dublín. Soy irlandesa. *i* Hola. Me llamo Ernesto. Soy de Gerona. Soy español.

Unit 2

1 **Masculine**
un café té vino jerez coñac cava gin tonic zumo de naranja cortado zumo de tomate

Feminine
una tónica cerveza gaseosa coca-cola **un** agua mineral (**una** changes to **un** before **agua**, even though the word is feminine)

2 C: Buenos días. ¿Qué van a tomar?
M: Para mí, **una** cerveza, por favor.
L: Para mí, **un** vino tinto.
J: **El** vino, ¿es español?
C: ¡Claro!
J: Para mí, **un** vino blanco, entonces.
C: ¿Y usted?
E: Yo quiero **un** té.
C: Entonces, **una** cerveza, **un** vino tinto, **un** vino blanco y **un** té. ¿Quiere **el** té con leche?
E: No, con limón.
C: Ahora mismo.

3 C: ¿**La** tónica?
S: Para mí, por favor.
C: ¿Y **el** zumo de tomate?
S: Para mí.
C: ¿Y **el** café con leche?
S: Para mí.

4 *a* encantada *b* ésta amiga *c* éste el hermano vecina *d* mi novia encantado *e* cuñado inglés *f* Éste el tío *g* Éste mi marido *h* padre

5 *a* 2 *b* 3 *c* 1 *d* 3 *e* 1 *f* 2

6 Te presento a mi familia. **Ésta** es mi madre, Teresa, y **éste** es mi padre, Ernesto. Y **éste** es mi hermano, Luis y su mujer, Mercedes. Y **ésta** es mi hermana, Lola y su hijo Francisco, con un amigo, Tomás. Y **ésta** es la novia de Francisco, se llama Inés.

Unit 3

1 *a* quesos   *b* panes   *c* jamones
d lechugas   *e* patatas   *f* aceitunas
g huevos   *h* plátanos   *i* melones
j tomates

2 *a* Los hijos de Mercedes   *b* Los amigos de
Ana   *c* Las hermanas de Pablo   *d* Las
amigas de Paco   *e* Los primos de Juana
f Las sobrinas de Luisa

3 *a* Juana tiene un primo.   *b* Pablo tiene una
hermana.   *c* Luisa tiene una sobrina.
d Mercedes tiene un hijo.   *e* Paco tiene
una amiga.   *f* Ana tiene un amigo.

4 *a* El hijo de Mercedes se llama Roberto.
b El amigo de Ana se llama Jorge.   *c* La
hermana de Pablo se llama Marta.   *d* La
amiga de Paco se llama Marisa.   *e* El primo
de Juana se llama Javier.   *f* La sobrina de
Luisa se llama Isabel.

5 *a* (No additional words required)
b Póngame medio kilo de patatas, por
favor.   *c* (No additional words required)
d También quiero una lechuga.   *e* (No
additional words required)   *f* Póngame un
cuarto de kilo de jamón de York y dos
botellas de agua.

6 *a* una botella **pequeña** de leche   *b* ½ kilo
de queso **manchego**   *c* 1 kilo de plátanos
maduros   *d* dos latas **grandes** de sardinas
e una bolsa de patatas **fritas**   *f* 2 tónicas
frescas   *g* 100 gramos de jamón **serrano**
h un yogur **desnatado**

7 *a* tiene   *b* tienes   *c* tengo   *d* tienen
e tienes   *f* tiene

8 *a* veinte   *b* cinco   *c* dos   *d* cien
e doscientos cincuenta   *f* un
g cuatrocientos   *h* diez   *i* doce
j mil ochocientas

Unit 4

1 *a* ¿Dónde está el Hotel Calatrava, por
favor?   *b* ¿Dónde está la plaza mayor, por
favor?   *c* ¿Dónde está la farmacia, por
favor?   *d* ¿Dónde está la oficina de
turismo, por favor?   *e* ¿Dónde están los
servicios, por favor?   *f* ¿Dónde están los
jardines públicos, por favor?

2 Siga **por** la calle Calabria y **a** la derecha está
la oficina municipal **de** turismo. Enfrente **de**
la oficina hay un garaje. **En** la segunda calle
a la izquierda está el piso **de** mi amiga.
Enfrente **de** su piso está el hotel y todo
recto, llega usted **a** la plaza. **A** diez minutos
andando está el parque, **a** un kilómetro, más
o menos.

3 *a* una botella de leche   *b* medio kilo de
manzanas   *c* está al final de la calle
d Alejandro es del Perú   *e* Toledo está a
setenta kilómetros de Madrid

4 *a* está   *b* es   *c* está está   *d* está es
e está

5 *a* él   *b* usted/él/ella   *c* tú   *d* ella
e usted/él/ella   *f* yo   *g* usted

6 *a* Coja la primera calle a la izquierda y al
final a la derecha está el hotel. (**Derecha** and
izquierda are interchangeable.)   *b* La
catedral está a cien metros en la plaza
enfrente de la oficina de turismo.   *c* Coja la
segunda calle a la derecha, todo recto y el
bar está a la izquierda.   *d* Lo siento, no soy
de aquí.   *e* El museo está a veinte minutos
andando.   *f* La oficina de turismo está en el
centro cerca de la estación. (**Estación** and
oficina de turismo are interchangeable.)

Unit 5

1 *a* Sí, estoy de vacaciones.   *b* No, estoy
estudiando.   *c* Sí, estoy paseando.   *d* No,
estoy trabajando.   *e* Sí, estoy tomando el
sol.   *f* Sí, pero estoy aprendiendo español.

2 *b* Está estudiando.   *c* Está paseando.
d Está trabajando.   *e* Está tomando el sol.
f Está aprendiendo español.

3 *a* Hablo italiano bastante bien.   *b* Bailo el
«rock» muy mal.   *c* Marta toca el piano
muy bien.   *d* Hablo inglés bastante mal.
e Mi hermano nada regular.   *f* Mi amiga
canta mal.

4 *a* Hablo italiano . . .   *b* Bailo el «rock» . . .
c Toco el piano . . .   *d* Hablo inglés . . .
e Nado . . .   *f* Canto . . .

5 *a* No, no estoy trabajando aquí.   *b* No, no
hablo francés bien.   *c* No, no tengo hijos.
d No, no vivo en un piso.   *e* No, no estoy
de vacaciones este mes.   *f* No, no soy
español.

6 *a* le   *b* me   *c* te   *d* te   *e* me   *f* le

7 *a* gustan   *b* gustan   *c* gusta   *d* gusta
e gustan   *f* gustan   *g* gusta

8 *a* moderno   *b* pintorescos   *c* tinto
barato   *d* muy limpia   *e* tranquilo
f porque son divertidas   *g* extranjeros

Unit 6

1 *a* está *b* están *c* hay *d* hay *e* está
f está

2 *a* de jamón *b* de vino tinto/leche *c* de
tuti fruti *d* de té *e* de vino tinto/leche
f de patatas fritas *g* de chocolate

3 En la calle
A: Perdone, ¿**hay** una gasolinera **por** aquí?
B: No lo sé, lo siento, no soy **de** aquí.
A: Perdone, ¿**hay una** gasolinera cerca?
C: Sí, **a** doscientos metros.
A: ¿**Dónde** está exactamente?
C: **En** la primera **calle** a la derecha, **está**
delante del banco.

En la gasolinera
A: Lleno, por favor . . . ¿**hay/tiene/n** planos
de la ciudad?
D: Sí, **en** la tienda, al lado **de** los servicios.

4 *a* ø *b* ¿Hay manzanas? *c* ø *d* Lo siento,
no hay jamón serrano. *e* ø *f* ¿Hay mapas
de carreteras?

5 *a* España tiene muchas catedrales famosas.
b En Madrid hay restaurantes muy caros.
c En esta discoteca hay un ambiente muy
divertido. *d* Esta carretera no tiene
gasolineras. *e* En las oficinas de turismo
hay mucha información útil. *f* Esta ciudad
tiene muchos parques muy bonitos.

6 1 *b* 2 *a* 3 *b* 4 *a* 5 *c* 6 *a*

Unit 7

1 *a* Son las dos menos cuarto. *b* Son las
diez y media. *c* Son las doce y cinco.
d Es la una. *e* Es la una y veinte. *f* Son
las once y cuarto. *g* Son las ocho menos
diez. *h* Son las cuatro menos cuarto.

2 *a* A las ocho y media de la noche. *b* A las
nueve y media de la mañana. *c* A las siete
y media de la tarde. *d* A las ocho de la
mañana. *e* A las cinco de la tarde. *f* A las
ocho de la noche. *g* A las nueve de la
mañana. *h* A las ocho de la noche.
i A las diez de la noche.

3 *a* A las cuatro y media. *b* A la una. *c* Sí,
por la mañana y por la tarde. *d* No, no
trabaja por la tarde. *e* No, no trabaja por la
mañana. *f* Termina a las dos. *g* No, no
trabaja por la mañana.

4 *a* trabajas *b* trabajo *c* empiezo
d tienes *e* termino *f* vive *g* vivo
h habla *i* habla

5 *a* un hospital *b* profesor/a *c* Soy
agricultor/a *d* trabajo en un hospital
e una empresa *f* es secretaria/oficinista
g es electricista *h* trabaja en una fábrica
i Soy profesor/a

6 electricista (m/f) contable (m/f) arquitecto
(m) mujer de negocios (f) diseñador (m)
escritora (f) ingeniera (f) dentista (m/f)
jefe (m) profesor (m)

Unit 8

1 *a* ¿Qué va/n a tomar? *b* ¿Y de postre?
c ¿Y para beber? *d* ¿Qué tal el lomo?
e ¿Qué es la tortilla a la paisana? *f* ¿Qué
hay/tienen para comer? *g* ¿Dónde están
los servicios? *h* ¿Qué hay de tapas?
i ¿Qué quieren beber? *j* ¿El agua con gas
o sin gas?

2 *a* Para mí/quiero una ración de tortilla
española. *b* De primero, sopa de verduras.
c De segundo, pollo con patatas fritas.
d Para beber, una botella de agua mineral
sin gas y una cerveza. *e* De postre, fruta.
f De segundo, calamares. *g* Para beber,
una jarra de agua. *h* De postre, peras al
vino y . . . la cuenta.

3 *a* ¡Sí!, ¡está buenísima! *b* ¡Sí!, ¡están
sabrosísimos! *c* ¡Sí!, ¡está riquísima!
d ¡Sí!, ¡está saladísimo! *e* ¡Sí!, ¡están
cocidísimas! *f* ¡Sí!, ¡están buenísimas!
g ¡Sí!, ¡es baratísimo! *h* ¡Sí!, ¡es
carísimo! *i* ¡Sí!, ¡es dificilísima!

4 *a* empiezo *b* quiero *c* prefieres
d quiere *e* prefiero *f* cierra *g* piensas
h recomienda

5 1 *a* 2 *a* 3 *b* 4 *a* 5 *b* 6 *a* 7 *c*

6 (The version that follows is not meant to be
prescriptive: you may not have included *all*
these points, or followed this order.)

El primo de Mercedes se llama Ignacio.
Tiene treinta y cinco años. No tiene hijos.
Vive en Valencia, en una casa grande en las
afueras. No le gustan los pisos del centro.
Trabaja en un hospital: es médico. Le gusta
muchísimo su trabajo. Empieza a las dos de
la tarde y termina a las diez de la noche. Le
gusta Valencia porque es grande,
interesante y tiene mucho ambiente. Le
gusta salir a comer a los restaurantes de la
ciudad. No le gusta la carne. Le gustan
muchísimo los platos de pescado,
especialmente la paella. Habla inglés y
también italiano. No le gustan los animales.

7 Mercedes
le gusta Burgos la carne
le gustan los pisos en el centro
los restaurantes las ciudades pequeñas
no le gusta el pescado
no le gustan las ciudades grandes

Ignacio
le gusta Valencia la paella el italiano
le gustan las ciudades grandes
los restaurantes
no le gustan los pisos en el centro
los animales

Unit 9

1 *a* me parecen muy cómodos *b* me parece
muy elegante *c* me parece caro *d* me
parece pequeña *e* me parecen muy
bonitas *f* me parecen baratos

2 *a* te parece *b* le parecen *c* le parece
d te parecen *e* le parecen

3 *a* me la llevo *b* me los llevo *c* me lo
llevo *d* me las llevo *e* me la llevo *f* me
lo llevo *g* me lo llevo

4 *a* quiero el estampado *b* quiero el gris
c quiero la blanca *d* quiero los blancos
e quiero las rojas *f* quiero la celeste
g quiero el verde

5 *a* Me llevo éste porque es baratísimo.
b Me llevo ésta porque es baratísima.
c Me llevo éste porque es baratísimo.
d Me llevo éste porque es baratísimo.
e Me llevo ésta porque es baratísima.

6 *a* ¿A qué hora se cierra el supermercado los
sábados? *b* ¿A qué hora se abre la
farmacia el lunes por la mañana? *c* ¿A qué
hora se abre el supermercado? *d* ¿A qué
hora se cierra El Drugstore los sábados?
e ¿A qué hora se cierra la farmacia por la
noche?

7 *a* 3 *b* 4 *c* 5 *d* 8 *e* 6 *f* 7 *g* 1 *h* 2

Unit 10

1 *b* Sí, soy aficionado al golf. *c* Sí, soy
aficionado a la natación. **2** *a* Soy
aficionada a la lectura. *b* Soy aficionado a
la música moderna. *c* Soy aficionado a la
cocina. **3** *a* Soy aficionado al cine. *b* Soy
aficionada al teatro. *c* Soy aficionada
al arte.

2 In this exercise anything is acceptable,
provided you have something from each
column.

3 *a* Me gusta comer en un restaurante, pero
prefiero comer en casa. *b* Me gusta mucho
nadar en el mar, pero prefiero nadar en la
piscina. *c* Me gusta hablar italiano, pero
prefiero hablar español. *d* Me gusta ir al
cine, pero prefiero ir al teatro. *e* Me gusta
bailar, pero prefiero escuchar música.
f Me gusta leer revistas, pero prefiero leer
novelas.

4 *a* Esta tarde voy a leer novelas. *b* ¿Esta
noche vas a cocinar? *c* María Cubells va a
hacer footing hoy. *d* Esta mañana voy a
hacer atletismo. *e* ¿Esta semana vas a (ir a)
alguna exposición? *f* Hoy voy a comer en
este restaurante chino. *g* Esta tarde voy a
hacer natación/nadar.

5 *a* duermo puedo *b* juegas *c* puede
d vuelves *e* vuelvo *f* cuesta *g* duerme
h cuesta

6 *a* Marisa juega al golf. *b* Juan juega al
fútbol. *c* Marta María juega al waterpolo.
d Jorge juega al baloncesto. *e* Pepa juega
al tenis. *f* Javier juega al ajedrez.

7 *a* tengo *b* estás *c* estoy *d* hace *e* eres
f tienes *g* hago *h* es

Unit 11

1 *a* ¿A qué hora sale el tren para Valencia?
b ¿Cómo se llega a la plaza Gaudí, por
favor? *c* ¿Este autobús va a la Gran Vía?
d ¿Quiere un billete de ida o de ida y
vuelta? *e* ¿De dónde sale el autobús
número treinta? *f* ¿Hay trenes a Sevilla
por la tarde después de las seis? *g* Éste es
el tren para Córdoba, ¿verdad?

2 *a* está *b* llega *c* coge prefiere *d* sale
e es *f* tiene *g* viene *h* viaja

3 *a* . . . está en la farmacia también.
b . . . hace mucha natación también.
c . . . siempre coge el tren de las dos y cinco
también. *d* . . . es estudiante también.
e . . . llega a casa a las siete también.
f . . . trabaja nueve horas al día también.
g . . . viene en tren también.
h ¡ . . . tiene mucho trabajo también!

4 *a* las dieciocho cuarenta (18:40) *b* las
doce treinta (12:30) *c* las seis cero cinco
(06:05) *d* las diecinueve cincuenta y cinco
(19:55) *e* las veintitrés quince (23:15)
f las dieciséis veinticinco (16:25) *g* las
diez cero dos (10:02)

5 *a* a qué hora (3)   *b* cuándo (5)
c dónde (2)   *d* de dónde (7)
e cuánto (6)   *f* cuántos (4)   *g* cómo (1)

6 *a* ¿Hay un autobús para Tarragona?
b ¿Hay una gasolinera cerca?
c ¿Hay algo para los turistas en Ávila?
d ¿En Tarragona hay murallas antiguas?
e ¿Hay una farmacia por aquí?
f ¿Hay una playa limpia en esta costa?

7 1 es 2 gusta 3 a 4 donde 5 gustan
6 por 7 coger 8 y 9 sale 10 de
11 llega 12 las 13 es 14 va 15 casa

Unit 12

1 *a* tenemos *b* vivimos *c* tenemos
d comemos *e* somos estamos *f* vamos
g aparcamos *h* practicamos

2 *a* vamos a salir. *b* aceptamos tarjetas de
crédito. *c* los dejamos/dejamos nuestros
pasaportes. *d* no llevamos (equipaje).
e firmamos. *f* somos.

3 *a* ¿Tienen un menú del día? *b* ¿Aceptan
tarjetas de crédito? *c* ¿Tienen ascensor?
d ¿Reservan billetes de autocar?
e ¿Alquilan patines? *f* ¿Dónde venden
bebidas/refrescos? *g* ¿Cambian monedas
extranjeras? *h* ¿Abren los sábados?

4 *a* 2 *b* 2 *c* 3 *d* 1 *e* 2 *f* 3

5 *a* ¿Se puede aparcar? *b* ¿Se puede entrar?
c ¿Se puede comer en este parque? *d* ¿Se
puede telefonear? *e* ¿Se puede dejar las
joyas en recepción? *f* ¿Se puede
desayunar en la habitación? *g* ¿Se puede
ir a la discoteca?

6 *a* ø *b* se *c* ø *d* ø *e* se *f* se *g* ø
h ø

7 **En el centro de la ciudad**
se puede . . .   *a* comprar en tiendas más
baratas
b ir a muchos espectáculos
c trabajar cerca de casa
d salir de noche con
frecuencia
e visitar monumentos y
museos

En las afueras
se puede . . .   *f* respirar aire puro
g jugar en calles sin tráfico
h descansar sin ruido
i salir al campo
j ver el paisaje

Unit 13

1 *a* En Madrid hace sol. *b* No, llueve/está
lloviendo y hace viento. *c* En Londres,
llueve/está lloviendo. *d* No, hace frío.
e En Roma hace calor. *f* En Berlín nieva/
está nevando.

2 *a* terminan *b* pasas *c* firma *d* reservo
e ocupa *f* venden *g* aparco *h* tomáis
i visitamos *j* desayunan

3 *a* comemos *b* trabajo *c* compran
d llega *e* estudiáis *f* miras

4

Yo	hago	muchas fotos
		excursiones a pie
Mi marido	vamos	a las cuatro
y yo		cada día
		al cine
	venimos	a las cuatro
		cada día
		al cine
		aquí con
		frecuencia
		de Valencia
Los amigos	hacen	excursiones a pie
de Juan		muchas fotos
	son	muy simpáticos
		de Valencia
La hermana	viene	a las cuatro
de Javi		cada día
		al cine
		aquí con
		frecuencia
		de Valencia
Tú	das	el pasaporte
		a la policía
Ustedes	hacen	excursiones a pie
		muchas fotos
	son	muy simpáticos
		de Valencia
Vosotros	estáis	aquí con
		frecuencia
	tenéis	muchas fotos

5 *a* me duele la espalda *b* me duele la
cabeza *c* me duelen las muelas *d* me
duele el estómago *e* me duele la garganta
f me duelen los oídos

6 *a* tengo dolor de espalda *b* tengo dolor de
cabeza *c* tengo dolor de muelas *d* tengo
dolor de estómago *e* tengo dolor de
garganta

7 *a* En La Coruña llueve más/En Toledo llueve menos *b* En los Pirineos nieva más/En Valencia nieva menos *c* En Oviedo hace menos sol/En Córdoba hace más sol *d* En Madrid en agosto hace más calor/En octubre hace menos calor *e* En Londres hace más frío en invierno/En Barcelona hace menos frío en invierno *f* En Menorca hace más viento/En Segovia hace menos viento

8 *a* El bocadillo de atún es mejor que el (bocadillo) de queso. *b* La camisa azul es más pequeña que la (camisa) amarilla/la camisa amarilla es más grande que la (camisa) azul. *c* El jamón de York es más barato que el (jamón) serrano/el jamón serrano es más caro que el (jamón) de York. *d* El restaurante 'La Concha' es mejor que (el restaurante) 'El Toro Bravo'. *e* Correos está más lejos que la farmacia/la farmacia está más cerca que Correos. *f* El Hotel Nuria es mejor que (el Hotel) 'El Faro'. *g* Tomás es más alto que Felipe/Felipe es menos alto que Tomás.

Unit 14

1 *a* El año pasado estuve de vacaciones en México. *b* ¿Adónde fuiste el año pasado? *c* El año pasado fui a Torremolinos. *d* Y ¿adónde fue Joaquín el año pasado? *e* Luisa estuvo en Manresa una semana el año pasado. *f* ¿Estuviste trabajando en verano el año pasado? *g* María fue de vacaciones en tren el año pasado. *h* ¿Cuánto tiempo estuviste en la montaña el año pasado?

2 *a* El fin de semana pasado . . . *b* Ayer . . . *c* La semana pasada . . . *d* El año pasado . . . *e* El mes pasado . . . *f* El verano pasado . . .

3 *a* ¿Adónde piensas/quieres ir el año que viene? *b* Pienso/quiero ir al Perú. *c* ¿Qué país piensa/quiere usted visitar en este viaje? *d* Pienso/quiero pasar una semana en la playa. *e* ¿Y qué pensáis/queréis hacer? *f* Pensamos/queremos tomar el sol. *g* ¿Piensas/quieres ir al cine? ¿Qué piensas/quieres ver? *h* ¿Piensan/quieren viajar el próximo verano?

4 Present: *a f g* Past: *b c i* Future: *d e h j*

5 *a* no me gustó *b* te gusta *c* le gusta *d* me gusta/gustó *e* no me gustó *f* te gustó *g* me gustó

6 **El Norte de España**
me gustó porque: es verde y limpio, tiene un pescado excelente y es una zona tranquila; **pero no me gustó:** el tiempo: llueve mucho y hay tormentas.

El Pirineo
me gustó porque: el paisaje es bonito, la comida es buena, hay mucha pesca y se puede hacer alpinismo; **pero no me gustó:** el ambiente por la noche y es difícil viajar por la zona sin coche (hay malas comunicaciones).

Extremadura
me gustó porque: hay ciudades históricas, ruinas romanas; **pero no me gustó:** el tiempo: hace mucho calor y el paisaje es muy seco, y no me gustó la miseria.

Unit 15

1 *a* 1 está 2 tiene 3 hay *b* 1 tiene/tienen 2 quiere 3 están 4 quiere 5 hay 6 hay *c* 1 se puede 2 se puede

2 *a* llevo *b* cierra *c* tengo *d* tienen *e* vivís *f* hacemos *g* empieza *h* coméis *i* volvemos

3 *a* ¿Cómo estás?/¿Qué tal? *b* ¿Cómo te llamas/se llama? *c* ¿Cuántos hermanos tienes/tiene? *d* ¿Cuántos años tienen? *e* (Hola) Buenas tardes. *f* Te presento a/Éste es/Ésta es . . . *g* ¿Qué va/van a tomar? *h* ¿Algo más? *i* ¿De dónde eres/es?

4 C: **Medio kilo** de manzanas, por favor.
D: ¿Algo más?
C: Sí, **cien gramos** de queso manchego, **una lata** de sardinas, **una bolsa** de patatas fritas y **una botella** de vino blanco.
D: ¿Eso es todo? Son **mil cuatrocientas pesetas**.

5 *a* 5 *b* 3 *c* 7 *d* 2 *e* 6 *f* 1 *g* 9 *h* 4 *i* 8

6 Conchita Fuentes vive en Vilasar, un pueblo cerca de Barcelona. Tiene treinta y siete años. Es casada: su marido se llama Wolfgang y es alemán. Tiene una hija que se llama Ingrid y tiene cinco años. Conchita es psicóloga. Trabaja en casa. Los lunes, miércoles y viernes empieza a las nueve de la mañana y trabaja hasta la una. Todos los días trabaja por la tarde: empieza a las dos y termina a las ocho. Le gusta la música clásica y la cocina vegetariana. También le gusta tocar la guitarra y el piano, leer y hacer yoga. Siempre va de vacaciones a Alemania. Conchita es miembro de un grupo 'verde'.

7 *a* Me gusta más el pescado. *b* El verde es más caro. *c* En febrero hace más frío. *d* ¿Tiene una más barata? *e* Prefiero la (bolsa) grande. *f* De primero, la paella es mejor que las verduras. *g* Prefiero la primavera. *h* Por la tarde los españoles hacen la siesta.

8 *a* de *b* por *c* por *d* de *e* por *f* de

9 *a* pasando *b* saliendo *c* comiendo *d* entrando *e* cruzando *f* viviendo *g* aprendiendo *h* tomando

10 *a* Sí, me lo llevo. *b* Sí, me los llevo. *c* Sí, me lo llevo. *d* Me la llevo. *e* Sí, me las llevo. *f* Sí, me lo llevo. *g* ¡Sí!, me lo llevo. *h* Sí, me lo llevo.

11 *a* el dolor de estómago *b* ¿Tiene algo para el dolor de cabeza? *c* las quemaduras de sol *d* ¿Tiene algo para el dolor de garganta? *e* comida para bebés *f* crema bronceadora

12 *a* 4 *b* 5 *c* 8 *d* 7 *e* 2 *f* 1 *g* 3 *h* 6

Key to multiple-choice test

1 *c* 2 *b* 3 *b* 4 *a* 5 *a* 6 *c* 7 *b* 8 *c*
9 *a* 10 *b* 11 *a* 12 *c* 13 *b* 14 *c* 15 *a*
16 *b* 17 *c* 18 *c* 19 *b* 20 *a* 21 *b* 22 *c*
23 *b* 24 *a* 25 *b* 26 *c* 27 *c* 28 *b*
29 *a* 30 *b*

Score

21–30 Well done! Not only do you understand Spanish but you can distinguish between very similar words and realise that these distinctions are important for grasping the meaning and making yourself clearly understood.

14–20 You have learned a great deal but could improve your accuracy by going over the questions you did not get right trying to work out why your answers did not fit. Concentrate on the verb endings and other slight changes in spelling: they are important for getting the meaning across!

8–13 You have grasped enough of the grammar to get the gist of what people are saying. So far so good, but you need a little more practice if you want to get beyond simple questions and answers.

0–7 You may be able to cope with simple 'survival' situations such as shopping and ordering meals, but you will need more practice to master enough Spanish for a meaningful conversation. Don't give up! It's amazing how much easier it is the second time round.

List of exercises

References are to the Unit in which the exercise appears, followed by the number of the exercise.

Glossary

The following is a list of new words which do not appear in the *España Viva* course book:

a pie	*on foot, walking*	maduro/a	*ripe*
adelantado	SEE por adelantado	más de	*more than*
el aire puro	*fresh air*	multinacional	*multinational*
al día	*per day*	el pañuelo	*handkerchief, (fine) scarf*
el alpinismo	*rock climbing*	el papel	*paper* SEE *servilleta de papel*
alquilar	*to hire, rent, rent out*	el paquete	*packet*
alto/a	*tall*	el pariente	*relative*
el atún	*tuna*	el pastel	*cake*
la barra	*(long thin) loaf of bread*	el patín	*pedalo*
el bolsillo	*pocket*	la pesca	*fishing*
la bufanda	*(woollen) scarf*	pintoresco/a	*picturesque*
cambiar	*to change*	el plato	*dish*
cerrar con llave	*to lock*	el plato combinado	*mixed platter (as a set meal)*
la cocina vegetariana	*vegetarian cookery*	la plaza mayor	*main square*
cómodo/a	*comfortable*	poner	*to put*
el cuchillo	*knife*	por adelantado	*in advance*
chino/a	*Chinese*	precioso/a	*very pretty*
demasiados/as	*too many*	preparado/a	*ready*
directo/a	*through (train)*	el programa	*programme*
el disco	*record*	el/la psicólogo/a	*psychologist*
el dolor de muelas	*tooth-ache*	puro/a	SEE *aire puro*
el ejercicio	*exercise*	rápido/a	*fast*
elegante	*smart, elegant*	recomendar (**ie**)	*to recommend*
enérgico/a	*energetic*	respirar	*to breathe*
entonces	*then*	el «rock»	*Rock 'n' Roll*
el/la escritor/a	*writer*	el ruido	*noise*
estampado/a	*patterned*	las ruinas romanas	*Roman remains*
excelente	*excellent*	ruso	*Russian (language)*
el fuego	*light*	sabroso/a	*tasty*
las gafas de sol	*sunglasses*	salado/a	*salty*
hacer la siesta	*to have a nap*	seco/a	*dry*
histórico/a	*historic*	la servilleta de papel	*paper napkin*
el hueso	*bone*	servir	*to serve*
ir de camping	*to go camping*	sin alcohol	*alcohol-free, low alcohol*
ir de excursión	*to go on an outing*	sirven	SEE *servir*
ir de vacaciones	*to go on holiday*	el tráfico	*traffic*
ir de viaje	*to go on a trip*	la taza	*cup*
los juegos de mesa	*board games*	tocar la guitarra	*to play the guitar*
largo/a	*long*	la tormenta	*storm*
la lata	*tin, can*	útil	*useful*
lo siento	*I'm sorry*	vegetariano/a	*vegetarian*
la llave	SEE cerrar con llave		